THE WI BOOK OF
BISCUITS

WI BOOKS

ACKNOWLEDGEMENTS

Illustrated by Ann Rees
Edited by Sue Jacquemier and Rosemary Wadey
Designed by Clare Clements
The publishers would also like to thank
Cumbria-Westmorland and Cumbria-Cumberland
Federations of Women's Institutes for supplying recipes
for this book, and Sally Lister and Pat Hesketh for their
advice and contributions.

Published by WI Books Ltd.,
39, Eccleston Street,
London SW1W 9NT

British Library Cataloguing in Publication Data
The WI book of biscuits. — 2nd ed.
  1. Cookies
  641.8'654   TX772

  ISBN 0-900556-85-4

First impression 1984

Filmset by
D. P. Media Limited, Hitchin, Hertfordshire

Reproduced, printed and bound in Great Britain by
Hazell Watson & Viney Limited,
Member of the BPCC Group,
Aylesbury, Bucks

CONTENTS

Introduction 4

All sorts of biscuits 6
Plain and fancy biscuits of all kinds,
with a variety of flavourings.

Biscuits with chocolate 34
Chocolate-topped or
chocolate-flavoured, in different
shapes and sizes.

Oat biscuits 44
Made with oats or rolled in oats,
combined with all sorts of other
ingredients.

Nut biscuits 52
Walnuts, hazelnuts, almonds and
peanuts feature in a delicious range of
nut cookies.

Traditional and foreign biscuits 68
Everything from Cornish ginger
fairings to Passover meringues.

Savoury biscuits 82
Plain biscuits for cheese, tangy party
snacks and wholemeal titbits.

What is the WI? 93

Index 94

INTRODUCTION

Bake a batch of biscuits and just watch them dis-appear. Homemade biscuits and cookies have a spe-cial aroma and taste all of their own which is fit to tempt many a palate.

Biscuits are simple to prepare and make, and work out very much cheaper than their bought equival-ents. Oats, chocolate, nuts, and many other ingre-dients are used to create familiar biscuits and lots of new flavours are to be found in this book. It includes many traditional types, a selection of foreign tastes and a lot of everyday biscuits which can be prepared in a matter of minutes.

Use fresh ingredients, not the leftovers from the back of the cupboard, which may be stale and would not enhance the flavour or allow the biscuits to keep in good condition for any length of time. Butter will give a better flavour than other fat but it is not strictly necessary. Biscuits should keep well for 2–3 weeks in an airtight container but it must be really airtight and the lid replaced securely each time it is opened. Once baked, biscuits should be cooled rapidly and not left around for too long before storing.

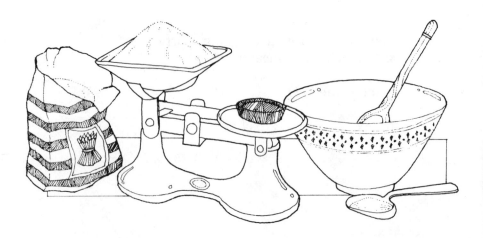

Measurements

All the spoon measures in this book are level unless stated otherwise.

3 tsp = 1 tbsp
8 tbsp = 5 fl oz = 150 ml = ¼ pint

Eggs are size 2 unless stated otherwise.

When following these recipes please use either the metric measurements or the imperial: do not mix them and all will be well.

Measurements for can sizes are approximate.

American equivalents

	Metric	Imperial	American
Butter, margarine	225 g	8 oz	1 cup
Shredded suet	100 g	4 oz	1 cup
Flour	100 g	4 oz	1 cup
Currants	150 g	5 oz	1 cup
Sugar	200 g	7 oz	1 cup
Syrup	335 g	11½ oz	1 cup

An American pint is 16 fl oz compared with the imperial pint of 20 fl oz. A standard American cup measure is considered to hold 8 fl oz.

ALL SORTS OF BISCUITS

Biscuits can be eaten at any time of the day.
Some are plain, some fancy, some full of fruit,
others topped with icing. The selection
here shows the versatility of the biscuit,
with lots of old friends and a good selection of
new ones too.

COCONUT KISSES

Makes about 24

100 g (4 oz) plain flour
pinch of salt
½ tsp baking powder
50 g (2 oz) caster sugar
50 g (2 oz) margarine
1 egg yolk
a little milk

Topping
1 egg white
50 g (2 oz) caster sugar
100 g (4 oz) desiccated coconut
glacé cherries (optional)

Heat the oven to 180°C (350°F) mark 4. For the biscuits: sift the flour, salt and baking powder together. Mix in the sugar and then rub in the fat until the mixture resembles fine breadcrumbs. Add the beaten egg yolk and a little milk if necessary, to form a dough. Roll out the dough on a floured board and cut out shapes with a 4-cm (1½-inch) cutter. Place on greased baking sheets.

For the topping: whisk the egg white until it is stiff. Add the sugar and whisk again. Fold in the coconut. Spread the mixture on to each biscuit and top with a quarter of a cherry if liked. Bake for 25–30 minutes until the biscuits are evenly browned. Cool on a wire rack.

ALPHABET BISCUITS

225 g (8 oz) plain flour
pinch of salt
¼ tsp ground cinnamon
150 g (5 oz) butter
50 g (2 oz) caster sugar
1 tbsp water
caster sugar to glaze

Icing
100 g (4 oz) icing sugar
1 tbsp water
food colouring (optional)

Heat the oven to 180°C (350°F) mark 4. For the biscuits: sift the flour, salt and cinnamon into a bowl, and rub in the butter until the mixture resembles fine breadcrumbs. Stir in the sugar, add the water and mix to a pliable dough. Knead until smooth.

Roll out thinly on a floured board, cut into small squares and place on lightly greased baking sheets. Brush with water and sprinkle with caster sugar to glaze. Bake for 15–20 minutes and cool on a wire rack.

For the icing: mix the sifted icing sugar with the water and beat to a smooth consistency; if liked, add a drop or two of liquid food colouring. Pipe letters on to each biscuit and leave to set.

GIPSY CRISPS

75 g (3 oz) cornflakes
225 g (8 oz) self-raising flour
100 g (4 oz) sugar
150 g (5 oz) margarine
2 tbsp golden syrup
1 tsp bicarbonate of soda
2 tsp boiling water

Heat the oven to 150°C (300°F) mark 2. Crush the cornflakes and mix them with the sifted flour and the sugar. Melt the margarine and syrup and add to the dry mixture. Finally, dissolve the bicarbonate of soda in boiling water and add to the mixture. Knead together to form a dough.

Roll the dough into small round balls and place on greased baking sheets. Bake for 20–25 minutes. Cool on a wire rack.

GROUND RICE COOKIES

100 g (4 oz) self-raising flour
100 g (4 oz) ground rice
100 g (4 oz) caster sugar
100 g (4 oz) margarine
1 egg, beaten
sugar for coating

Heat the oven to 180°C (350°F) mark 4. Sift the flour into a bowl and mix in the ground rice and sugar. Rub the margarine into the dry ingredients until the mixture resembles fine breadcrumbs then work into a dough with the beaten egg. Roll the dough into small balls and dip in the sugar.

Place on greased baking sheets and flatten slightly with a fork. Bake for 15–20 minutes. Cool on a wire rack.

ORANGE COCONUT CRISPS

Makes about 15

75 g (3 oz) butter or margarine
50 g (2 oz) caster sugar
grated rind of 1 orange
50 g (2 oz) plain flour
25 g (1 oz) cornflour
pinch of salt
orange juice
desiccated coconut

Heat the oven to 180°C (350°F) mark 4. Cream the fat and sugar until light and fluffy, then beat in the grated orange rind. Add the sifted flour, cornflour and salt and mix to form a dough.

Shape the dough into about 15 small balls. Brush each one with orange juice and roll in the coconut. Place on greased baking sheets and flatten slightly. Bake for 18 minutes. Cool on a wire rack.

NAPOLEON BISCUITS

100 g (4 oz) plain flour
25 g (1 oz) cornflour
65 g (2½ oz) margarine
40 g (1½ oz) caster sugar
1 egg yolk
jam, any flavour
icing sugar

Heat the oven to 200°C (400°F) mark 6. Sift the flour and cornflour into a bowl and rub in the fat until the mixture resembles fine breadcrumbs. Add the sugar and bind the mixture to a soft dough with the egg yolk.

Roll the dough out on a floured board to a thickness of 5 mm (¼ inch). Cut out rounds and remove their middles to make rings. Cut out an equal number of rounds the same size as the rings. Place on greased baking sheets and prick the rounds only. Bake for 10–15 minutes and cool on a wire rack.

When they are cold, spread the rounds with jam. Dust the rings with icing sugar and place on top of the jam.

CARAWAY BISCUITS

100 g (4 oz) margarine
50 g (2 oz) icing sugar, sifted
175 g (6 oz) self-raising flour, sifted
1 tsp caraway seeds
a little milk

Heat the oven to 180°C (350°F) mark 4. Cream the margarine and icing sugar together until light and creamy, then add the flour and caraway seeds. Mix to form a stiff dough adding a little milk if necessary. Roll the dough out on a floured board to 5 mm (¼ inch) thick and cut into shapes. Place on lightly greased baking sheets and bake for 15 minutes or until golden brown. Cool on a wire rack.

CHERRY WHIRLS

Makes 16–18

175 g (6 oz) butter
50 g (2 oz) icing sugar, sifted
1 tsp vanilla essence
175 g (6 oz) plain flour, sifted
8–9 glacé cherries

Heat the oven to 160°C (325°F) mark 3.
Cream the butter until it is light and soft.
Add the icing sugar and vanilla essence and
beat until smooth, then stir in the flour.
 Transfer the mixture to a large piping bag
fitted with a large star nozzle. Pipe 16–18
fairly small whirls on to two greased baking
sheets and top each one with half a cherry.
Bake in the centre of the oven for
20 minutes, or until a pale gold.
 Leave on the baking sheets for 5 minutes
before transferring carefully to a wire rack.
Store in an airtight container when cold.

COCONUT BISCUITS

50 g (2 oz) butter
75 g (3 oz) caster sugar
1 egg
75 g (3 oz) plain flour
25 g (1 oz) desiccated coconut

Heat the oven to 160°C (325°F) mark 3.
Cream the butter and sugar together until
light and fluffy, beat in the egg then fold
into the mixture followed by the flour and
the coconut. Put teaspoons of the mixture
on greased baking sheets and bake for
10–15 minutes. Cool on a wire rack.

NOVELTY BISCUITS

50 g (2 oz) margarine
50 g (2 oz) caster sugar
100 g (4 oz) self-raising flour
pinch of salt
15 g (½ oz) shelled walnuts,
 chopped
2 tsp desiccated coconut
15 g (1 oz) glacé cherries, chopped
4 tsp beaten egg

Heat the oven to 180°C (350°F) mark 4.
Cream the margarine and sugar until light
and fluffy. Sift the flour and salt and mix
with the nuts and coconut. Gradually add,
together with the cherries, to the creamed
mixture. Bind the dough together with the
egg. Roll it out on a floured board and cut
into shapes.
 Place on greased baking sheets and bake
for 15–20 minutes. Cool on a wire rack.

HIGHLANDERS

Makes about 20

100 g (4 oz) butter
50 g (2 oz) icing sugar
75 g (3 oz) self-raising flour
75 g (3 oz) plain flour
25 g (1 oz) demerara sugar

Heat the oven to 180°C (350°F) mark 4. Cream the butter and sifted icing sugar until they are very light. Sift the flours together and work in to make a dough; knead thoroughly. Form the mixture into a sausage and roll in the demerara sugar. Wrap in cling film or foil, place on something flat and put in the refrigerator for at least 1 hour.

Cut into 5-mm (¼-inch) slices, and place the biscuits on ungreased baking sheets. Bake for about 10 minutes. Be careful that the edges do not burn. Remove to a wire rack and leave to cool.

ICED GINGER SHORTCAKE

150 g (5 oz) plain flour
1 tsp baking powder
1 tsp ground ginger
100 g (4 oz) butter or margarine
50 g (2 oz) caster sugar

Icing
100 g (4 oz) caster sugar
50 g (2 oz) butter or margarine
1 tbsp golden syrup
1 tsp ground ginger.

Heat the oven to 160°C (325°F) mark 3. Sift the flour, baking powder and ginger together in a bowl. Cream the butter and sugar until light and fluffy. Mix the dry ingredients into the creamed mixture to make a dough.

Spread the mixture in a well greased 20-cm (8-inch) square tin and cook for 45 minutes until golden brown.

Meanwhile, prepare the icing by heating all ingredients together over a low heat. Pour over the shortcake while it is still hot. Cut it into fingers before it cools. Leave in the tin until cold.

COFFEE KISSES

225 g (8 oz) self-raising flour
75 g (3 oz) margarine
75 g (3 oz) caster sugar
1 egg
½ tsp coffee essence or about 2 tsp instant coffee powder

Filling
50 g (2 oz) butter
100 g (4 oz) icing sugar
1 tsp coffee essence or 1 tsp instant coffee powder dissolved in 1 tsp hot water

Heat the oven to 180°C (350°F) mark 4. For the biscuits: sift the flour into a bowl then rub in the margarine until the mixture resembles fine breadcrumbs; add the sugar. Mix in the beaten egg and coffee flavouring to make a dough. Roll the dough into small balls and place on greased baking sheets. Bake for 15–20 minutes and cool on a wire rack.

To make the filling: cream the butter until it is soft then gradually beat in the sifted icing sugar. Add the coffee flavouring and beat well.

When the biscuits are cold, sandwich together with the filling.

LEMON CRESCENTS

grated rind and juice of ½ lemon
50 g (2 oz) caster sugar
50 g (2 oz) butter
100 g (4 oz) plain flour
1 egg, beaten
chopped almonds

Heat the oven to 180°C (350°F) mark 4. Rub the grated lemon rind and the sugar in a basin until the sugar is yellow. Rub the butter into the sifted flour until it resembles fine breadcrumbs. Add the lemon juice and sugar and sufficient egg to bind together.

Roll the dough out thinly on a floured board and cut into crescent shapes. Place on a greased baking sheet. Brush with the remaining beaten egg and sprinkle with chopped almonds. Bake for 20 minutes. Cool on a wire rack.

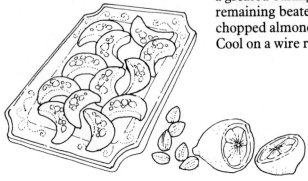

EASTER BUNNY BISCUITS

75 g (3 oz) soft margarine
100 g (4 oz) caster sugar
1 egg
225 g (8 oz) plain flour
pinch of salt
2 tsp mixed spice
25 g (1 oz) currants

Coating
egg white
desiccated coconut

extra currants to decorate

Heat the oven to 190°C (375°F) mark 5. Cream the fat and sugar until light and fluffy. Beat in the egg thoroughly, then fold in the sifted flour, salt, and spice. Add the currants and mix well to form a dough.

Roll the dough out on a floured board to a thickness of 5 mm (¼ inch). Cut out the biscuits with a rabbit-shaped cutter. Brush with egg white and dip in the coconut. Add a currant to each one to represent an eye.

Place the biscuits on greased and floured baking sheets and bake the biscuits near the top of the oven for 15–18 minutes. Remove carefully to a wire rack and leave to cool.

GINGER RUFFLES

100 g (4 oz) self-raising flour
½ tsp bicarbonate of soda
1 tsp ground ginger
50 g (2 oz) margarine
50 g (2 oz) caster sugar
2 tbsp golden syrup

Heat oven to 180°C (350°F) mark 4. Sift the flour, soda and ginger into a bowl. Rub in the margarine until the mixture resembles fine breadcrumbs, then add the sugar. Warm the syrup, add to the mixture and work well together.

Divide the dough into two pieces and form each one into a long sausage. Place each one in the middle of a greased baking sheet. Bake at the top of the oven for about 20 minutes. Remove from the oven and cut into strips while still warm. Cool the biscuits on a wire rack.

GINGER SNAPS

100 g (4 oz) margarine
4 tbsp golden syrup
225 g (8 oz) plain flour
pinch of salt
1 tsp ground ginger
100 g (4 oz) caster sugar
1 egg yolk
½ tsp bicarbonate of soda
a little milk
caster sugar

Heat the oven to 190°C (375°F) mark 5.
Melt the margarine and the syrup together
in a pan. Sift the flour, salt and ginger into a
bowl and stir in the sugar. Blend in the
melted margarine and syrup and the beaten
egg yolk. Dissolve the soda in a little warm
milk and add to the mixture.

Turn the dough on to a floured board and
knead until smooth. Roll out thinly on a
sugared board and cut into rounds about
6 cm (2½ inches) in diameter. Place on
greased and floured baking sheets and bake
for 15–20 minutes. Allow to set on the
baking sheet then remove to a wire rack and
leave to cool.

ORANGE CREAMS

Makes about 12 pairs

100 g (4 oz) margarine
100 g (4 oz) caster sugar
2 tsp golden syrup
finely grated rind of 1 small orange
1 egg yolk
150 g (6 oz) plain flour
25 g (1 oz) custard powder
½ tsp cream of tartar
½ tsp bicarbonate of soda

Filling
40 g (1½ oz) butter
75 g (3 oz) icing sugar, sifted
a little grated orange rind
about 1 tsp orange juice

Grease two or three baking sheets. Heat the
oven to 190°C (375°F) mark 5. Cream the
margarine and sugar together until very
light and fluffy. Beat in the syrup, orange
rind and egg yolk. Sift the flour, custard
powder, cream of tartar and soda together
and work into the creamed mixture.

Roll the mixture into balls the size of a
small walnut and put on to the baking
sheets allowing room for spreading. Bake
for about 20 minutes or until golden brown.
Remove carefully to a wire rack and leave to
cool.

For the filling: cream the butter and
sugar together, then beat in the orange rind
and sufficient orange juice to give a thick
spreading consistency. Use the orange
butter cream to sandwich the biscuits
together when they are cool.

PEANUT BUTTER COOKIES

1 tbsp peanut butter
grated rind of ½ orange
50 g (2 oz) butter
50 g (2 oz) caster sugar
3 tbsp soft light brown sugar
1 egg, beaten
100 g (4 oz) self-raising flour

Heat the oven to 180°C (350°F) mark 4. Cream the peanut butter, orange rind, butter and both sugars until the mixture is light and fluffy. Work in the beaten egg and stir in the sifted flour to make a firm dough.

Roll the dough into walnut-sized pieces and place, spaced well apart, on greased baking sheets. Dip a fork in a little flour and press criss-cross lines on top of each one. Bake for 25 minutes until risen and golden brown. Cool on a wire rack.

RICE BISCUITS

225 g (8 oz) self-raising flour, sifted
100 g (4 oz) ground rice
175 g (6 oz) caster sugar
175 g (6 oz) margarine
4 tbsp milk
¼ tsp lemon essence
glacé cherries

Heat the oven to 180°C (350°F) mark 4. Mix the flour, rice and sugar together in a bowl. Rub in the margarine until the mixture resembles fine breadcrumbs. Mix to a stiff dough with the milk and lemon essence.

Roll the dough out thinly on a floured board and cut into rounds with a plain or fluted cutter 6 cm (2½ inches) in diameter. Decorate each one with a small piece of cherry. Place on greased baking sheets and bake for about 15 minutes, then cool on a wire rack.

COCONUT CRISPS

225 g (8 oz) self-raising flour, sifted
225 g (8 oz) soft margarine
75 g (3 oz) icing sugar
drop of vanilla essence
25 g (1 oz) desiccated coconut

Heat the oven to 160°C (325°F) mark 3. Cream all the ingredients together except the coconut. Form the mixture into small balls and roll in the coconut. Place on greased baking sheets and bake for about 20 minutes or until they are golden brown. Cool on a wire rack.

RICH BISCUITS

Makes about 40

225 g (8 oz) self-raising flour
100 g (4 oz) caster sugar
100 g (4 oz) margarine or butter
grated rind and juice of ½ lemon
1 egg, beaten

Heat the oven to 180°C (350°F) mark 4. Sift the flour into a bowl and mix in the sugar. Rub in the margarine until the mixture resembles fine breadcrumbs. Add the grated lemon rind and mix to a stiff dough with the beaten egg and lemon juice.

Roll the dough out thinly on a floured board and cut into approximately 40 rounds with a scone cutter about 5 cm (2 inches) in diameter. Bake for about 15 minutes. Cool on a wire rack.

SWEETMEAL COOKIES

Makes 16–18

75 g (3 oz) wholemeal flour
15 g (½ oz) plain flour
pinch of salt
½ tsp baking powder
15 g (½ oz) fine oatmeal
40 g (1½ oz) butter or margarine
40 g (1½ oz) caster sugar
about 2 tbsp milk

Grease two baking sheets. Heat the oven to 190°C (375°F) mark 5. Mix the wholemeal flour with the sifted plain flour, salt and baking powder in a bowl and add the oatmeal. Add the butter and rub in until the mixture resembles fine breadcrumbs. Stir in the sugar and add sufficient milk to mix to a stiff paste. Knead well.

Roll out thinly on a lightly floured surface and cut into rounds using a plain or fluted 5 or 6-cm (2 or 2½-inch) cutter. Transfer to the baking sheets and prick well all over. Bake for 15–20 minutes or until a light golden brown. Cool on a wire rack and store in an airtight container.

Variation
If made small they may be sandwiched together with a flavoured butter cream.

FRUITY SNAPS

50 g (2 oz) sultanas
25 g (1 oz) caster sugar
50 g (2 oz) margarine
4 tbsp golden syrup
150 g (5 oz) self-raising flour, sifted

Heat the oven to 180°C (350°F) mark 4. Place the sultanas, sugar, margarine and syrup in a pan and warm over a low heat until the fat melts. Take care that the mixture does not overheat. Remove from the heat, add the flour and beat well.

Place small tablespoons of the mixture well apart on greased baking sheets. Bake for about 12–15 minutes until golden brown. Allow to set before removing from the baking sheets, but do not leave for too long or they will stick. Cool on a wire rack.

COFFEE COOKIES

Makes 20–25

75 g (3 oz) butter
50 g (1½ oz) caster sugar
½ tsp almond essence
100 g (4 oz) self-raising flour, sifted
1 tsp instant coffee powder
2 tsp water

Icing
½ tsp instant coffee powder
2 tsp warm water
3 tbsp icing sugar sifted
a few decorations (optional)

Grease two baking sheets. Heat the oven to 180°C (350°F) mark 4. Cream the butter, sugar and essence together until very light and fluffy, then gradually work in the flour. Dissolve the coffee in the water and add to the mixture to form a pliable dough.

Divide the mixture into 20–25 equal pieces and roll into balls. Place on the baking sheets and flatten with a fork. Alternatively roll out the dough thinly on a lightly floured board and cut into shapes using a variety of biscuit cutters; place on the baking sheets.

Bake in the centre of the oven for 15–20 minutes until just firm. Remove carefully with a palette knife and cool on a wire rack.

For the icing: dissolve the coffee powder in the water and gradually beat in the icing sugar until smooth. Put a small amount on to each biscuit and if liked top with a piece of walnut, crystallized violet or rose petal, etc., and leave to set.

APRICOT SHORTCAKES

175 g (6 oz) plain flour
100 g (4 oz) butter
50 g (2 oz) ground rice
50 g (2 oz) caster sugar
40 g (1½ oz) apricot jam
extra jam for decoration
extra caster sugar

Heat the oven to 180–190°C (350–375°F) mark 4–5. Sift the flour into a bowl and rub in the butter until the mixture resembles fine breadcrumbs. Add the ground rice and sugar and mix together. Put the jam in the centre of the mixture and work into a smooth dough.

Roll out on a floured board to about 2 cm (¾ inch) thick. Cut into fancy shapes. Place on greased baking sheets. Make a small hollow in the centre of each biscuit with a thimble and put a little jam in the hole. Bake for about 20 minutes. Cool on a wire rack and when the biscuits are cold, dredge with caster sugar.

BASIC DROP COOKIES

75 g (3 oz) margarine
75 g (3 oz) caster sugar
1 egg, beaten
225 g (8 oz) plain flour
½ tsp baking powder
3 tbsp milk
½ tsp vanilla essence

Heat the oven to 180°C (350°F) mark 4. Cream the margarine and sugar until light and fluffy then add the beaten egg. Sift the flour and baking powder together and add to the creamed mixture alternating with the milk and vanilla essence. Not all the milk may be needed as the mixture must not be too soft.

Drop teaspoons of the mixture on to a greased baking sheet, leaving room for the biscuits to spread. Bake for 10–16 minutes, then cool on a wire rack.

Variations
(1) Substitute soft brown sugar for caster sugar to make a light brown cookie.
(2) Fruit and nut cookie: add 75 g (3 oz) dried fruit and 25 g (1 oz) chopped nuts.
(3) Cinnamon wafer: add 1 tsp ground cinnamon to the dry ingredients.

(4) Chocolate wafer: substitute 1 tbsp cocoa for 25 g (1 oz) flour.

All the cookies may be iced and decorated.

CARAWAY MOMENTS

Makes 30

75 g (3 oz) butter or margarine
75 g (3 oz) lard or white fat
125 g (5 oz) light soft brown sugar
1 egg, beaten
275 g (10 oz) self-raising flour,
    sifted
1 tsp vanilla essence
½ tsp caraway seeds
about 50 g (2 oz) cornflakes,
    crushed
8 glacé cherries, quartered

Grease two or three baking sheets. Heat the oven to 180°C (350°F) mark 4. Beat the fats together until well blended, add the sugar and cream together until light and fluffy. Beat in the egg then gradually mix in the flour, essence and caraway seeds to give a fairly stiff dough.

Divide the mixture into 30 pieces and roll each into a ball. Roll in the crushed cornflakes and place fairly well apart on the baking sheets. Flatten each slightly and top each one with a piece of glacé cherry. Bake for 15–20 minutes or until golden brown. Cool on a wire rack and store in an airtight container.

GINGER BISCUITS

100 g (4 oz) margarine
100 g (4 oz) caster sugar
1 tbsp treacle
1 tbsp golden syrup
225 g (8 oz) self-raising flour
1 tsp ground ginger
1 tsp bicarbonate of soda
a little hot water

Heat the oven to 180°C (350°F) mark 4. Cream the margarine and sugar until light and fluffy. Warm the treacle and syrup and add to the creamed mixture with the sifted flour and ginger. Dissolve the soda in a little hot water and stir into the mixture. Mix thoroughly.

Roll the dough into balls and place on greased baking sheets. Bake for 15 minutes. Cool on a wire rack.

ICED RASPBERRY BISCUITS

75 g (3 oz) margarine
75 g (3 oz) caster sugar
1 egg
200 g (7 oz) plain flour
pinch of salt

Filling
raspberry jam

Icing
100 g (4 oz) icing sugar
1 tbsp water

Heat the oven to 200°C (400°F) mark 6. Cream the margarine and sugar until light and fluffy then beat in the egg. Sift the flour and salt into the mixture and knead together. Roll out the dough on a lightly floured board and cut into rounds with a medium-sized cutter. Place on greased baking sheets and bake for 8–10 minutes. Cool on a wire rack. When cold, sandwich together with the raspberry jam.

To make the icing: mix the sifted icing sugar with the water and beat to a smooth consistency. Spread the icing over the tops of the biscuits and leave to set.

FREEZER BISCUITS

1 egg, beaten
200 g (7 oz) caster sugar
200 g (7 oz) plain flour
1 tsp baking powder
½ tsp salt
100 g (4 oz) butter or soft margarine

Mix together the egg and sugar. Sift the flour into a bowl with the baking powder and salt and add any flavouring (see variations). Melt the butter or use soft margarine and add this to the mixture to make a soft dough.

Knead lightly, then form into a sausage shape 2.5 cm (1 inch) in diameter. Wrap in greaseproof paper or cling film and place in the freezer or refrigerator until needed. Defrost if frozen until soft enough to cut. Cut off slices about 5 mm (¼ inch) thick and place on greased baking sheets. Bake for 15–20 minutes at 180°C (350°F) mark 4. Cool on a wire rack.

Variations
(1) 1 tsp vanilla essence and 50 g (2 oz) chopped walnuts.
(2) 1 tsp almond essence and 50 g (2 oz) chopped almonds.
(3) 1 tsp ground ginger and 50 g (2 oz)

chopped crystallized or stem ginger.
(4) 50 g (2 oz) grated chocolate and 1 tsp
vanilla essence.
(5) 1 tbsp instant coffee powder and 50 g
(2 oz) chopped walnuts.
(6) Grated rind of 1 lemon and 50 g (2 oz)
currants.
(7) 1 tsp vanilla essence and 1 tbsp instant
coffee powder.
(8) Use soft brown sugar instead of caster
sugar and add 1 tsp vanilla essence and 50 g
(2 oz) chopped raisins.

RAISIN SHORTCAKE

4 tbsp orange juice
100 g (4 oz) seedless raisins
175 g (6 oz) plain flour
100 g (4 oz) butter
50 g (2 oz) caster sugar

Heat the oven to 180°C (350°F) mark 4. Put
the orange juice and raisins into a pan and
bring slowly to the boil. Leave to cool. Sift
the flour into a bowl and rub in the butter
until the mixture resembles fine
breadcrumbs. Add the sugar and knead the
dough well, then divide it into two equal
portions.

Shape each piece into a round and place
one on a greased baking sheet. Spread with
the raisin mixture and top with the second
round; press firmly together. Prick well all
over and bake for 30 minutes. Mark into
sections. Remove from the baking sheet
when cold and break up into pieces.

CRISPS

Makes about 36

175 g (6 oz) margarine
100 g (4 oz) soft brown sugar
100 g (4 oz) self-raising flour
1 tsp baking powder
100 g (4 oz) bran buds

Heat the oven to 180°C (350°F) mark 4.
Cream the margarine and sugar together
until light and fluffy. Sift the flour and
baking powder and add to the mixture
followed by the bran buds. Knead together
to form a dough.

Roll the dough into small balls and place
on greased baking sheets. Bake for about
15 minutes or until golden brown. Cool on a
wire rack.

BURNT BUTTER BISCUITS

100 g (4 oz) butter
100 g (4 oz) caster sugar
1 egg, beaten
175 g (6 oz) self-raising flour

Heat the oven to 180°C (350°F) mark 4. Put
the butter in a saucepan and cook until it is
golden brown. Pour into a bowl and leave it
to cool. When the butter has just set, mix in
the sugar and beat well. Add the egg and
then gradually work in the sifted flour to
make a stiff dough.

Roll the dough into small balls, place on
greased baking sheets and bake for about
15 minutes. Cool on a wire rack.

COCONUT RINGS

Makes 16–18

100 g (4 oz) plain flour
100 g (4 oz) caster sugar
100 g (4 oz) butter or margarine
100 g (4 oz) desiccated coconut
1 egg, beaten
raspberry jam

Lightly grease two baking sheets. Heat the
oven to 190°C (375°F) mark 5. Sift the flour
into a bowl and mix in the sugar. Add the
fat and rub in until the mixture resembles
breadcrumbs, then stir in the coconut. Bind
to a fairly soft but manageable dough with
the egg.

Knead the dough lightly and roll out
thinly on a floured surface. Cut into rounds
using a 6-cm (2½-inch) plain or fluted

cutter, then stamp out the centres using a 2.5-cm (1-inch) cutter. Put the rings on a baking sheet. Re-roll the trimmings and cut out more rings.

Bake for about 15 minutes or until lightly tinged brown. Cool on a wire rack and when cold sandwich together in pairs with the raspberry jam.

YO-YO'S

175 g (6 oz) margarine
50 g (2 oz) icing sugar, sifted
175 g (6 oz) self-raising flour
50 g (2 oz) custard powder
½ tsp vanilla essence

Filling
50 g (2 oz) butter
100 g (4 oz) icing sugar
2–3 drops vanilla essence

Heat the oven to 180°C (350°F) mark 4. For the biscuits: cream the margarine and icing sugar until light and fluffy. Work in the sifted flour and custard powder followed by the vanilla essence.

Roll the dough into balls and place on greased baking sheets. Mark with the back of a fork. Bake for 10 minutes. Cool on a wire rack.

To make the filling: cream the butter until it is soft. Gradually beat in the sifted icing sugar and the vanilla essence and beat until smooth. Sandwich the biscuits together with the filling.

CINNAMON BARS

100 g (4 oz) margarine
75 g (3 oz) caster sugar
½ egg
125 g (5 oz) plain flour
2 tsp ground cinnamon
pinch of salt
chopped nuts

Heat the oven to 140°C (275°F) mark 1.
Cream the margarine and sugar until they
are light and fluffy. Beat in the egg,
reserving a little of the white for glazing.
Sift the flour, cinnamon and salt together
and gradually add to the creamed mixture.
  Press the dough into a greased oblong
tin approximately 18 x 28 cm
(7 x 11 inches). Brush the surface with egg
white and sprinkle with chopped nuts. Bake
for 1 hour. Cut into slices and allow to cool
in the tin, then remove carefully and store
in an airtight container.

CHESTNUT BISCUITS

100 g (4 oz) butter
100 g (4 oz) caster sugar
1 egg yolk
225 g (8 oz) plain flour, sifted
1 tsp chestnut purée, sweet or
  natural

Heat the oven to 150–160°C (300–325°F)
mark 2–3. Cream the butter and sugar until
light and fluffy. Add the egg yolk and flour
and lastly the purée. Knead together
thoroughly.
  Roll out the dough on a lightly floured
board and cut into rounds approximately
5 cm (2 inches) in diameter. Place them on
greased baking sheets and bake for
30 minutes or until they are golden brown.
Cool on a wire rack.

SEMOLINA PYRAMID BISCUITS

75 g (3 oz) butter
50 g (2 oz) sugar
50 g (2 oz) cornflour
25 g (1 oz) semolina
a little jam, any flavour

Heat the oven to 180°C (350°F) mark 4.
Cream the butter and sugar until light and
fluffy. Mix the cornflour and semolina and
add to the creamed mixture to form a
dough. Knead well.
  Roll the dough out thinly on a floured

board. Cut out equal numbers of rounds with a 2.5-cm (1-inch) fluted cutter, a 4-cm (1½-inch) plain cutter, and a 5-cm (2-inch) fluted cutter. Put the rounds on greased baking sheets and bake for 15 minutes. Cool on a wire rack.

When the biscuits are cold, sandwich the three rounds together with jam to form a pyramid.

KELVIN CRISPS

100 g (4 oz) plain flour
½ tsp ground cinnamon
½ tsp baking powder
100 g (4 oz) butter or margarine
75 g (3 oz) caster sugar
75 g (3 oz) desiccated coconut
1 egg, beaten

Heat the oven to 180°C (350°F) mark 4. Sift the flour, cinnamon and baking powder into a bowl, then rub in the fat until the mixture resembles breadcrumbs. Add the remainder of the dry ingredients and mix together with the well beaten egg to make a fairly stiff dough.

Roll the dough out on a lightly floured board to a thickness of 5 mm (¼ inch). Stamp out into small rounds and place on greased baking sheets. Bake for 15 minutes. Cool on a wire rack.

Variations
When they are cold, serve the biscuits:
(1) Topped with a dab of melted chocolate and half a glacé cherry.
(2) Sandwiched together with apricot jam.

COCONUT DROPS

2 egg whites
100 g (4 oz) granulated sugar
225 g (8 oz) desiccated coconut

Heat the oven to 180°C (350°F) mark 4.
Beat the egg whites until stiff and dry. Add
the sugar and coconut and beat them all
together.

Drop small teaspoons of the mixture on
to baking sheets lined with greased
greaseproof paper or non-stick parchment
and bake for about 20 minutes. Cool on a
wire rack.

HONEY BISCUITS

100 g (4 oz) unsalted butter
6 tbsp clear honey
50 g (2 oz) caster sugar
1 tsp bicarbonate of soda
1 egg yolk
100 g (4 oz) plain flour
100 g (4 oz) sugar lumps

Heat the oven to 200°C (400°F) mark 6.
Melt the butter and pour it into a large
bowl. As it begins to cool, stir in the honey,
caster sugar, soda and egg yolk. Add the
sifted flour gradually and mix to form a
firm dough.

Roll rounded teaspoons of the mixture
into balls on a floured board. Coarsely crush
the sugar lumps and dip the top of each ball
into it. Place the balls on baking sheets lined
with non-stick baking parchment and bake
for 12 minutes. Cool on a wire rack.

OATMEAL BISCUITS

150 g (5 oz) plain flour
1 tsp baking powder
175 g (6 oz) coarse oatmeal
100 g (4 oz) caster sugar
75 g (3 oz) butter
a little milk

Heat the oven to 150°C (300°F) mark 2. Sift
the flour and baking powder into a bowl,
and add the oatmeal and sugar. Rub the
butter into the dry ingredients, then add the
milk and mix to form a dough. Roll out the
dough on a lightly floured board and cut
into shapes. Place the biscuits on well
greased baking sheets and bake for
15–20 minutes. Cool on a wire rack.

WHOLEMEAL SHORTCAKE

100 g (4 oz) butter
50 g (2 oz) Barbados sugar
225 g (8 oz) plain wholemeal flour
pinch of salt
25 g (1 oz) ground almonds
½ egg yolk

Heat the oven to 160°C (325°F) mark 3.
Cream the butter and sugar until they are
soft and fluffy. Stir in the dry ingredients
then add the egg yolk and work together to
form a dough. Roll the dough out on a
floured surface and cut into pieces or rounds
approximately 6–7.5 cm (2½–3 inches) in
diameter. Bake for about 15–20 minutes.
Cool on a wire rack.

LEMON FUDGE BISCUITS

225 g (8 oz) plain 'tea' biscuits
50 g (2 oz) desiccated coconut
grated rind of ½ lemon
100 g (4 oz) butter or margarine
200 g (7 oz) condensed milk

Icing
a few drops of yellow food colouring
1½ tbsp lemon juice
175 g (6 oz) icing sugar

For the base: crush the biscuits (the easiest
way is to put the biscuits in a polythene bag
and crush with a rolling pin) then add the
coconut and lemon rind. Melt the butter
and add the condensed milk. Add to the dry
ingredients and mix thoroughly. Press the
mixture into a greased Swiss roll tin.

To prepare the icing: add the yellow food
colouring to the lemon juice and mix in the
sifted icing sugar. Spread the icing over the
base and leave to set. Cut the biscuits into
shapes.

DREAM COOKIES

100 g (4 oz) soft margarine
75 g (3 oz) caster sugar
150 g (5 oz) plain flour
pinch of salt
½ tsp baking powder
1–2 drops vanilla essence
blanched almonds

Heat the oven to 180°C (350°F) mark 4.
Cream the margarine and sugar until light
and fluffy. Sift the flour with the salt and
baking powder and work into the creamed
mixture with the vanilla essence.

Roll the dough into small balls, place on
greased baking sheets and top each one with
an almond. Bake for 15–20 minutes or until
pale gold. Cool on a wire rack.

AUNTIE DOT'S BISCUITS

Makes 18

75 g (3 oz) butter or margarine
75 g (3 oz) caster sugar
75 g (3 oz) self-raising flour, sifted
a little egg
75 g (3 oz) raisins
cornflakes

Heat the oven to 180°C (350°F) mark 4. Cream the fat and sugar until light and fluffy. Stir in the flour and about half a beaten egg or sufficient egg to make a very stiff dough, then knead in the raisins.

Roll teaspoons of the mixture into balls, then roll them in cornflakes. Place on greased baking sheets, leaving plenty of room for them to spread. Bake for about 12 minutes then cool on a wire rack.

BUTTER COOKIES

175 g (6 oz) butter
100 g (4 oz) soft brown sugar
225 g (8 oz) plain flour, sifted
25 g (1 oz) demerara sugar

Heat the oven to 180°C (350°F) mark 4. Cream the butter and the brown sugar until light and fluffy. Work in the flour to give a smooth dough. Divide in half and form each piece into a sausage shape, then roll each in the demerara sugar. Wrap in cling film or foil and cool in the refrigerator until they are quite firm.

Cut into slices and place on greased baking sheets. Bake for 20 minutes then cool on a wire rack.

COCONUT BUTTER BISCUITS

175 g (6 oz) butter
2 tbsp golden syrup
100 g (4 oz) desiccated coconut
225 g (8 oz) self-raising flour
½ tsp bicarbonate of soda
175 g (6 oz) caster sugar

Heat the oven to 180°C (350°F) mark 4. Melt the butter and syrup in a pan then add the coconut. Sift the flour and soda into the mixture and stir well. Lastly stir in the caster sugar.

Shape the dough into small balls, and place on greased baking sheets leaving room for the biscuits to spread. Bake for 12–15 minutes. Cool on a wire rack.

KRINGLES

Makes about 48

225 g (8 oz) plain flour
2 tsp baking powder
100 g (4 oz) butter
225 g (8 oz) caster sugar
1 egg
3 tbsp brandy
2 tsp caraway seeds
caster sugar for dredging

Heat the oven to 190°C (375°F) mark 5. Sift 175 g (6 oz) of the flour with the baking powder. Cream the butter and sugar until soft and then beat in the egg, brandy and caraway seeds. Stir in the sifted flour, then add enough of the remaining 50 g (2 oz) of flour to make a stiff dough that you can handle. Cover and chill thoroughly.

Roll the dough out on a floured board to a thickness of 2.5 mm (⅛ inch). Cut into shapes and put on ungreased baking sheets. Sprinkle with caster sugar and bake for 15 minutes. Cool on a wire rack.

CRUNCHY BISCUITS

100 g (4 oz) butter or margarine
75 g (3 oz) caster sugar
1 tbsp golden syrup
100 g (4 oz) self-raising flour, sifted
100 g (4 oz) rolled oats
pinch of salt
pinch of bicarbonate of soda

Topping
175 g (6 oz) cooking chocolate,
  plain or milk

Heat the oven to 180°C (350°F) mark 4.
Cream the butter, sugar and syrup together,
then mix in the dry ingredients. Roll the
dough into small balls. Place on greased
baking sheets and press flat with a fork.
Bake for 15–20 minutes. Cool on a wire
rack. When the biscuits are cold, cover with
melted chocolate.

CHRISTMAS TREE COOKIES

150 g (6 0z) butter
150 g (6 oz) caster sugar
1 egg, separated
grated rind of 1 orange
150 g (6 oz) plain flour
50 g (2 oz) self-raising flour
icing sugar to dust

Grease two or three baking sheets. Heat the
oven to 190°C (375°F) mark 5.
   Cream the butter until soft, add the sugar
and beat until light and fluffy. Reserve a
little egg white for glazing and add the rest
of the egg to the mixture. Beat in the orange
rind and fold in the sifted flours. Knead
lightly until smooth, wrap in cling film or
foil and chill for 30 minutes.
   Roll out the dough on a lightly floured
board to about 5 mm (¼ inch) thick. Cut
out Christmas tree shapes from thick card
about 9 cm (3½ inches) high or use a metal
cutter and cut out as many 'trees' as
possible, rerolling the pastry trimmings.
   Place the 'trees' on the baking sheets and
mark the branches with the prongs of a
fork. Brush lightly with egg white and bake
in the centre of the oven for 10–15 minutes
until a pale brown. Cool on a wire rack.
   The biscuits may be lightly dredged with
icing sugar to represent snow. Store in an
airtight container.

PINEAPPLE BUTTONS

Makes about 20 pairs

100 g (4 oz) butter
2 tbsp double cream
100 g (4 oz) plain flour
caster sugar
50 g (2 oz) butter
100 g (4 oz) icing sugar, sifted
1 egg yolk
*50 g (2 oz) glacé pineapple, finely
  chopped*

Prepare two ungreased baking sheets. Heat the oven to 190°C (375°F) mark 5. Cream the butter until very soft, then beat in the cream. Sift the flour and work into the mixture. Wrap in cling film or foil and chill for at least an hour.

Roll out the dough lightly on a floured board to about 3 mm (⅛ inch) thick. Cut into plain rounds using a 4-cm (1½-inch) cutter. Dredge both sides with sugar and place on the ungreased baking sheets. Prick with a fork and bake in the centre of the oven for about 10 minutes or until slightly puffy, but not browned. Cool on a wire rack.

For the filling: cream the butter and icing sugar until soft then beat in the egg yolk and glacé pineapple. Use to sandwich the biscuits together in pairs.

ORANGE MELTAWAYS

Makes about 40

225 g (8 oz) butter
50 g (2 oz) icing sugar, sifted
grated rind of 1 orange
225 g (8 oz) plain flour, sifted
4 tbsp apricot jam, sieved
1 tbsp water
2 tbsp icing sugar, sifted
a little orange or lemon juice

Grease two or three baking sheets. Heat the oven to 160°C (325°F) mark 3. Cream the butter until soft then add the icing sugar and beat together until blended. Beat in the orange rind then work in the flour. Place the mixture in a large piping bag fitted with a large star nozzle. Pipe about 40 shell shapes on to the baking sheets and chill for 30 minutes.

Bake for about 25 minutes or until slightly coloured. Remove from the oven and brush each cookie first with apricot glaze (apricot jam heated with water) and then with the icing sugar blended with a little orange juice to make a soft icing. Return to the oven for 5 minutes.

FRUITED GINGER BISCUITS

Makes 35–40

100 g (4 oz) butter or margarine
100 g (4 oz) demerara sugar
200 g (8 oz) plain flour
2 tsp ground ginger
1 tsp ground cinnamon
1 tsp bicarbonate of soda
50 g (2 oz) golden syrup, warmed
75 g (3 oz) currants
about 3 tbsp milk
blanched almonds

Grease two baking sheets. Heat the oven to 180°C (350°F) mark 4.

Cream the butter and sugar until light and fluffy. Sift together the flour, ginger, cinnamon and soda. Stir into the creamed mixture followed by the syrup, currants and sufficient milk to give a fairly soft dough.

Place teaspoons of the mixture on the baking sheets allowing plenty of room for them to spread. Place a blanched almond on each one and bake just above the centre of the oven for about 20 minutes or until well risen and browned.

Cool slightly on the baking sheet before removing carefully to a wire rack to cool. Store in an airtight container.

COCONUT WAFERS

Makes about 15

90 g (3½ oz) butter
100 g (4 oz) caster sugar
25 g (1 oz) long-shred coconut, roughly chopped
25 g (1 oz) angelica, roughly chopped
1 tsp flour
1 tbsp top of the milk

Line two baking sheets with non-stick parchment. Heat the oven to 180°C (350°F) mark 4.

Melt the butter in a small pan, add the sugar and boil for a minute or so stirring continuously. Remove from the heat and stir in the coconut, angelica, flour and milk.

Cool a little, then drop in small heaps well apart on to the baking sheets. Bake just above the centre of the oven for about 10 minutes or until golden brown.

Leave briefly until they begin to firm up and then lay over a greased rolling pin and leave until cold and firm. Repeat with the remaining mixture.

Store in an airtight container for up to a week.

BISCUITS WITH CHOCOLATE

The flavour of chocolate is many people's favourite. The biscuits and cookies here are all flavoured with chocolate in one way or another. Some are dipped or topped with chocolate, some have a chocolate filling, while others are made from a chocolate-flavoured dough.

CATHERINE WHEELS

Makes about 24

75 g (3 oz) butter
100 g (4 oz) caster sugar
½ egg
175 g (6 oz) plain flour
½ tsp baking powder
pinch of salt
1 tbsp cocoa powder
1 tsp milk
½ tsp vanilla essence

Heat the oven to 160°C (325°F) mark 3. Cream the butter and 75 g (3 oz) of the sugar until light and fluffy. Gradually beat in the egg. Sift together the flour, baking powder and salt then fold into the creamed mixture to make a soft dough. Divide the dough into two equal parts. Add the sifted cocoa and milk to one portion and work it in gently with the fingertips. Add the essence to the other portion.

Roll each piece into an oblong 25 x 15 cm (10 x 6 inches). Place the cocoa dough on top of the plain dough and roll up the two layers closely and firmly from one long side. Wrap the roll in foil or cling film and chill in the refrigerator for 30 minutes.

Grease two baking sheets. Cut the dough into 24 slices and place on the baking sheets. Bake in the centre of the oven for 15–20 minutes or until golden brown. Cool on a wire rack before dredging with the remaining caster sugar.

CHOCOLATE CHIP BISCUITS

100 g (4 oz) butter
100 g (4 oz) caster sugar
2 tbsp condensed milk
75 g (3 oz) plain chocolate
175 g (6 oz) self-raising flour

Heat the oven to 150°C (300°F) mark 2. Cream the butter and sugar together until light and fluffy, then beat in the condensed milk. Break or chop the chocolate into chips the size of sultanas and add to the creamed ingredients. Sift the flour and work into the mixture. Mix the dough well, then roll into walnut-sized balls.

Place on greased baking sheets and press down with a fork. Bake for 25–30 minutes or until golden brown. Cool on a wire rack.

DROP COOKIES

175 g (6 oz) plain flour
1 tsp bicarbonate of soda
pinch of salt
100 g (4 oz) butter or margarine
75 g (3 oz) caster sugar
25 g (1 oz) soft brown sugar
1 egg
a few drops of vanilla essence
100 g (4 oz) chocolate chips

Heat the oven to 160°C (325°F) mark 3. Sift together the flour, soda and salt. Cream the butter and both of the sugars in a basin until they are light and fluffy. Gradually beat in the light beaten egg and vanilla essence. Stir in half of the flour mixture, beat well to give a smooth dough, then add the remaining flour and the chocolate chips. Blend to form a smooth dough.

Take rounded teaspoons of the mixture and place on greased baking sheets – about 12 to a sheet. Bake for 12–15 minutes then lift carefully on to a wire rack so that they lie flat. Store the biscuits in an airtight container when cold.

CARAMEL BISCUITS

100 g (4 oz) butter
50 g (2 oz) caster sugar
175 g (6 oz) self-raising flour, sifted

Caramel
200-g (7-oz) can condensed milk
100 g (4 oz) margarine
50 g (2 oz) caster sugar
2 tbsp golden syrup
a few drops of vanilla essence

Topping
200 g (7 oz) chocolate (plain or milk)

Heat the oven to 180°C (350°F) mark 4. For the base: cream the butter and sugar until light and fluffy then mix in the flour. Press the dough into a greased rectangular tin 30 x 20 cm (12 x 8 inches) and bake for 15 minutes until golden brown. Leave to cool in the tin.

For the caramel: put all the ingredients in a pan and melt over a gentle heat. Bring to the boil and boil the mixture for 5 minutes, stirring all the time. Cool until it begins to thicken then pour over the base and leave to set.

For the topping: melt the chocolate in a basin over a pan of hot water and pour over the caramel. As it sets, swirl the top with a round-bladed knife. When quite set, cut into fingers.

CHOCOLATE BISCUITS

Makes about 24

75 g (3 oz) butter
175 g (6 oz) caster sugar
1 egg
1 tsp vanilla essence
175 g (6 oz) self-raising flour
1 tbsp cocoa powder
chocolate (plain or milk)

Heat the oven to 190°C (375°F) mark 5. Cream the butter and sugar until light and fluffy. Add the egg and vanilla essence and beat again. Sift the flour and cocoa together and work into the mixture.

Roll teaspoons of the dough into balls, place on a greased baking sheet and flatten slightly. Bake for about 15 minutes, then cool on a wire rack.

When the biscuits are cold, top with melted chocolate and leave to set.

COCONUT AND CHERRY SLICES

150 g (5 oz) cooking chocolate
50 g (2 oz) margarine
100 g (4 oz) caster sugar
1 egg
50 g (2 oz) glacé cherries
100 g (4 oz) desiccated coconut

Heat the oven to 170°C (335°F) mark 3–4. Line a Swiss roll tin with foil. Melt the chocolate in a bowl over a pan of hot water and then spread it over the foil and leave to cool.

Cream the margarine and sugar until light and fluffy then beat in the egg. Chop the cherries and fold in to the creamed mixture with the coconut. Spread this mixture over the cooled chocolate and bake for 15–20 minutes. Leave to cool in the tin and when the biscuit is cold, cut into slices. Store in an airtight container.

38

CHOCOLATE PEPPERMINT CREAMS

100 g (4 oz) butter
50 g (2 oz) caster sugar
½ tsp baking powder
1 tbsp drinking chocolate
100 g (4 oz) plain flour
75 g (3 oz) desiccated coconut

Filling
75 g (3 oz) butter
75 g (3 oz) icing sugar
¼ tsp peppermint essence
drop of green food colouring

Topping
100 g (4 oz) cooking chocolate

Heat the oven to 190°C (375°F) mark 5. For the base: cream the butter and sugar until light and fluffy. Sift the baking powder, drinking chocolate and flour together and add to the creamed mixture with the coconut. Press the mixture into a Swiss roll tin lined with greased greaseproof paper. Bake for about 15–20 minutes on the middle shelf of the oven until an even colour all over. Leave in the tin to cool.

For the filling: cream the butter and sugar until light and creamy then add the essence and colouring. Spread it evenly over the base.

Cover the layer of filling with the melted cooking chocolate and leave to set. Cut the biscuit into squares or fingers when the chocolate is firm.

CHOCOLATE QUICKIES

Makes 12–16

100 g (4 oz) butter or margarine
2 tbsp cocoa powder
1 tbsp demerara sugar
2 tbsp golden syrup
225 g (8 oz) semi-sweet biscuits, crushed
100 g (4 oz) plain or milk chocolate, broken up

Grease an 18-cm (7-inch) shallow square cake tin. Melt the butter in a small pan. Add the cocoa, sugar and syrup and when melted bring up to the boil. Boil for 1 minute. Remove from the heat and stir in the biscuit crumbs.

Turn the mixture into the tin and press in well to give a smooth top. Melt the chocolate in a basin over a pan of hot water, beat until smooth, then pour over the biscuit mixture. As the chocolate sets mark it into swirls with a round-bladed knife.

Chill until set firmly and then cut into squares or bars.

CHOCOLATE STARS

225 g (8 oz) plain flour
25 g (1 oz) cornflour
15 g (½ oz) cocoa powder
pinch of salt
100 g (4 oz) butter
100 g (4 oz) caster sugar
1 egg
½ tsp vanilla essence
2 tsp milk
50 g (2 oz) chococlate drops

Heat the oven to 160°C (325°F) mark 3. Sift the flour, cornflour, cocoa and salt into a bowl. Cream the butter and sugar until they are light and fluffy. Beat in the egg and vanilla essence. Work in the flour mixture and mix to a soft dough with the milk.

Put the mixture into a large forcing bag fitted with a large star nozzle. Pipe stars 4 cm (1½ inches) in diameter, spaced well apart, on greased baking sheets. Place a chocolate drop in the centre of each star and bake in the centre of the oven for 15 minutes. Cool on a wire rack.

CURLY PETERS

Plain mixture
100 g (4 oz) margarine
225 g (8 oz) plain flour, sifted
100 g (4 oz) caster sugar
1 tsp baking powder
1 egg, beaten

Chocolate mixture
100 g (4 oz) margarine
175 g (6 oz) plain flour, sifted with
    50 g (2 oz) cocoa powder
100 g (4 oz) caster sugar
1 tsp baking powder
1 egg, beaten

Heat the oven to 150–160°C (300–325°F) mark 2–3. For both mixtures: rub the margarine into the flour until the mixture resembles fine breadcrumbs, then add the sugar and baking powder. Bind them together with the egg to make a stiff dough.

Roll out each mixture separately on a floured board to the same size, then lay the chocolate mixture on top of the plain one. Roll up like a Swiss roll and cut the roll into 5-mm (¼-inch) slices. Lay on greased baking sheets and bake for 20–25 minutes or until pale brown. Cool on a wire rack.

CHOCOLATE CHERRY BISCUITS

Makes 18–20

100 g (4 oz) softened butter
50 g (2 oz) caster sugar
½ tsp vanilla essence
25 g (1 oz) glacé cherries
25 g (1 oz) plain chococlate
100 g (4 oz) plain flour, sifted

Heat the oven to 190°C (375°F) mark 5. Cream the butter and sugar until light and fluffy and then add the vanilla essence. Chop the cherries and the chocolate finely and add to the mixture; finally, work in the flour.

Place 18–20 teaspoons of the mixture on well greased baking sheets leaving space for the biscuits to spread. Bake for 15–20 minutes then cool on a wire rack.

CHERRY AND CHOCOLATE CHEWS

Makes 35

100 g (4 oz) butter
50 g (2 oz) caster sugar
2 tbsp condensed milk
175 g (6 oz) self-raising flour
pinch of salt
75 g (3 oz) plain cooking chocolate
50 g (2 oz) glacé cherries

Heat the oven to 180°C (350°F) mark 4. Cream the butter and sugar until light and fluffy then beat in the milk. Sift in the flour and salt. Chop the chocolate and cherries into small pieces and fold through the mixture.

Take good teaspoons of the mixture and roll into balls. Place on a greased baking sheet and flatten slightly. Bake for about 25 minutes. Cool on a wire rack.

CHOCOLATE WAGON WHEELS

100 g (4 oz) plain flour
pinch of salt
50 g (2 oz) margarine
25 g (1 oz) caster sugar
a few drops of vanilla essence
a little egg
25 g (1 oz) chocolate (plain or milk)

Heat the oven to 200°C (400°F) mark 6. Sift the flour and salt into a bowl and rub in the margarine until the mixture resembles fine breadcrumbs. Add the sugar and essence and mix to a dough with the beaten egg.

Roll the dough out on a lightly floured board and cut into 5-cm (2-inch) rounds with a plain cutter. Place on greased baking sheets and bake for about 10 minutes. Cool on a wire rack.

When the biscuits are cold, melt the chocolate over a pan of hot water. Dip each biscuit half-way into the chocolate and smooth its surface with a knife. Leave to set on a wire rack.

ICED PEPPERMINT BISCUITS

75 g (3 oz) plain flour
50 g (2 oz) butter
25 g (1 oz) sugar

Icing
a few drops of peppermint essence
a few drops of green food colouring
about 1 tbsp water
100 g (4 oz) icing sugar

Topping
225 g (8 oz) cooking chocolate
chocolate vermicelli

Heat the oven to 160°C (325°F) mark 3. Sift the flour into a bowl, rub in the butter until the mixture resembles breadcrumbs, then add the sugar. Knead until the mixture is smooth. Roll out thinly on a lightly floured board and cut into shapes. Place the biscuits on a greased baking sheet and bake for 10–15 minutes. Allow to cool before removing them from the baking sheet to a wire rack.

Prepare the icing by adding the peppermint essence and food colouring to the water. Mix in the sifted icing sugar and beat to a smooth consistency. Not all the water may be required as the icing should be quite thick. Spread the biscuits with the icing and leave to set.

Melt the chocolate over hot water and use to coat the biscuits, then decorate with the vermicelli. Leave to set.

QUICK FLORENTINES

175 g (6 oz) dates, chopped
50 g (2 oz) sultanas
100 g (4 oz) margarine
50 g (2 oz) caster sugar
50 g (2 oz) glacé cherries, chopped
25 g (1 oz) crystallized ginger, finely
  chopped
65 g (2½ oz) rice crispies
225 g (8 oz) cooking chocolate

Put the dates and sultanas in a saucepan with the margarine. Heat slowly, stirring all the time until soft. Add the sugar, cherries, ginger and rice crispies and stir well. Press the mixture into a Swiss roll tin and leave to set until firm.

Melt the chocolate in a bowl over hot water, and spread over the cooled mixture. Leave to set, then cut into bars.

CHOCOLATE MUESLI BISCUITS

75 g (3 oz) margarine
1 tbsp golden syrup
225 g (8 oz) muesli
50 g (2 oz) dates, chopped
50 g (2 oz) glacé cherries
100 g (4 oz) cooking chocolate

Melt the margarine and golden syrup together in a saucepan. Remove from the heat and stir in the muesli, dates and cherries. Press the mixture into a Swiss roll tin and leave to set.

Melt the chocolate in a bowl over hot water, and spread it over the cooled biscuit mixture. When set, cut into bars.

CHOCOLATE COCONUT KISSES

2 egg whites
100 g (4 oz) icing sugar
50 g (2 oz) desiccated coconut
100 g (4 oz) bitter chocolate,
  chopped

Heat the oven to 150°C (300°F) mark 2. Beat the egg whites stiffly, then add the icing sugar a little at a time, beating after each addition. Fold in the coconut and chocolate chips. Bake on an oiled baking sheet or a baking sheet lined with non-stick parchment, placing the mixture in small heaps.

Cook for 30 minutes until crisp.

GIPSY CREAMS

50 g (2 oz) lard
50 g (2 oz) margarine
50 g (2 oz) caster sugar
100 g (4 oz) self-raising flour, sifted
50 g (2 oz) rolled oats
1 tbsp chocolate or cocoa powder
2 tsp golden syrup dissolved in
   1 tbsp hot water

Filling
25 g (1 oz) butter
50 g (2 oz) icing sugar
1 tbsp chocolate powder
a few drops of vanilla essence

Heat the oven to 180°C (350°F) mark 4. For the biscuits: cream the lard, margarine and sugar until light and fluffy, then mix in all the other ingredients. Roll the dough into balls about the size of a large cherry.

Place on greased baking sheets and flatten with a fork which has been dipped in water. Bake for about 20 minutes, and leave on the baking sheets to cool.

To make the filling: cream the butter until it is soft. Gradually add the sifted icing sugar and beat until smooth. Add the chocolate powder and vanilla essence and beat well.

When the biscuits are cold, sandwich together in pairs with the filling.

OAT BISCUITS

Rolled oats add a delicious flavour and crunchiness to biscuits and cookies. Many of these recipes are made by melting the fat with sugar or syrup and kneading in the other ingredients. The biscuits are all crisp, crunchy and very 'moreish'.

ROLLED OAT BISCUITS

225 g (8 oz) butter or margarine
100 g (4 oz) soft brown sugar
175 g (6 oz) plain flour
75 g (3 oz) rolled oats
pinch of bicarbonate of soda
pinch of salt

Heat the oven to 150°C (300°F) mark 2. Cream the butter and sugar until soft then work in all the other ingredients. Roll the dough out on a floured board, but do not make it too thin. Cut into shapes and place on greased baking sheets. Cook for 20–25 minutes until golden brown. Cool on a wire rack.

COUPLAND BISCUITS

100 g (4 oz) butter or margarine
50 g (2 oz) caster sugar
1 tbsp golden syrup
100 g (4 oz) plain flour
50 g (2 oz) rolled oats
50 g (2 oz) desiccated coconut
1 tsp bicarbonate of soda
2 tsp hot water

Heat the oven to 180°C (350°F) mark 4. Beat the butter, sugar and syrup together until they are soft and creamy. Sift the flour and add to the mixture with the oats, coconut and the soda blended in the water; mix together to form a dough.

Roll the dough into small balls, place on greased baking sheets and flatten with a round-bladed knife. Bake for about 20 minutes or until golden brown. Cool on a wire rack.

OAT BISCUITS

100 g (4 oz) plain flour
1 tsp bicarbonate of soda
100 g (4 oz) rolled oats
100 g (4 oz) butter
100 g (4 oz) caster sugar
1 tbsp golden syrup
1 tbsp water

Heat the oven to 180°C (350°F) mark 4. Sift the flour and soda into a bowl and mix in the oats. Dissolve the butter, sugar and syrup in the water over a low heat, then stir into the dry ingredients.

Put teaspoons of the mixture on very well greased baking sheets, leaving room for the biscuits to spread. Bake on the top shelf of the oven for 15–20 minutes. Leave to cool for only a few seconds, then loosen with a palette knife. Cool on a wire rack.

TEBAY CRUNCH

225 g (8 oz) butter
100 g (4 oz) caster sugar
350 g (12 oz) rolled oats

Heat the oven to 180°C (350°F) mark 4.
Heat the butter and sugar in a pan until
melted, then add the oats gradually and mix
well together.

Turn the mixture into a greased
rectangular tin approximately 28 x 18 cm
(11 x 7 inches) and bake for 15–20 minutes
until lightly browned. Leave in the tin to
cool. Cut into pieces when cold.

BLANTYRE BISCUITS

100 g (4 oz) butter or margarine
100 g (4 oz) caster sugar
100 g (4 oz) rolled oats
100 g (4 oz) wholemeal flour
½ tsp baking powder
1 egg, beaten
2 bananas or 75 g (3 oz) chopped
  nuts

Heat the oven to 180°C (350°F) mark 4.
Cream the butter and sugar until light and
fluffy. Mix in the oats, flour and baking
powder. Add the egg and divide the dough
into two portions.

Put one half into a greased, shallow
20-cm (8-inch) square tin and press it down
with a fork. Spread the sliced bananas or
nuts over this and cover with the remaining
dough. Press it down firmly. Bake for
15–20 minutes or until golden brown. Cut
into fingers. Cool in the tin then remove
when cold and break up into fingers.

FIRELIGHTER BISCUITS

100 g (4 oz) margarine
1 tbsp golden syrup
225 g (8 oz) rolled oats
100 g (4 oz) brown sugar
25 g (1 oz) desiccated coconut
pinch of baking powder

Heat the oven to 180°C (350°F) mark 4.
Melt the fat and syrup together in a pan,
add the dry ingredients and mix together
thoroughly. Press the dough into a greased
Swiss roll tin so that it is 1 cm (½ inch)
thick. Bake for 20–30 minutes. Leave in
the tin and cut into fingers when it is cold.

CUMBERLAND SNAPS

100 g (4 oz) caster sugar
225 g (8 oz) margarine
2 tbsp golden syrup
1 tsp bicarbonate of soda
1 tbsp hot water
225 g (8 oz) plain flour
1 tsp ground ginger
50 g (2 oz) rolled oats

Heat the oven to 160°C (325°F) mark 3. Melt the sugar, margarine and syrup in a pan over a low heat. Dissolve the soda in the hot water. Sift the flour and ginger together and then mix together with all the other ingredients.

Roll the dough into small balls about the size of a walnut and place on greased baking sheets. Bake for 20–25 minutes until golden brown. Cool on a wire rack.

BUTTERCRUNCH

225 g (8 oz) self-raising flour
pinch of salt
175 g (6 oz) butter
2 tbsp golden syrup
175 g (6 oz) demerara sugar
100 g (4 oz) rolled oats

Heat the oven to 180°C (350°F) mark 4. Sift the flour and salt into a bowl and rub in the butter until the mixture resembles fine breadcrumbs. Add the syrup, sugar and oats and mix to form a firm dough. Break off pieces of dough the size of a walnut and roll into balls.

Place on greased baking sheets and flatten slightly. Bake for 15–20 minutes then cool on a wire rack.

ABBEY BISCUITS

Makes about 24

150 g (5 oz) margarine
150 g (5 oz) caster sugar
1 tbsp milk
1 tsp bicarbonate of soda
1 tsp golden syrup
150 g (5 oz) plain flour, sifted
100 g (4 oz) rolled oats

Heat the oven to 150°C (300°F) mark 2. Cream the margarine and sugar together, then add the milk, soda and syrup. Stir in the flour and oats and mix well. Roll the dough into small balls and space evenly apart on lightly greased baking sheets. Bake for 25 minutes until goden brown. Cool on a wire rack.

FLAKED ALMOND BISCUITS

Makes 48

100 g (4 oz) butter or margarine
100 g (4 oz) caster sugar
2 tsp black treacle
100 g (4 oz) self-raising flour, sifted
100 g (4 oz) rolled oats
25 g (1 oz) flaked almonds
1 tsp bicarbonate of soda
4 tbsp boiling water

Heat the oven to 180°C (350°F) mark 4. Cream the butter and sugar until light and fluffy. Add the treacle, then mix in the flour, oats and almonds. Dissolve the soda in the water and stir into the mixture to form a dough.

Roll teaspoons of the mixture into balls and place on greased baking sheets, allowing room for the biscuits to spread. Bake for 15 minutes. Cool on a wire rack.

CRUNCHIES

1 tsp bicarbonate of soda
1 tbsp tepid water
100 g (4 oz) margarine
1 tbsp golden syrup
100 g (4 oz) self-raising flour, sifted
100 g (4 oz) rolled oats
100 g (4 oz) granulated sugar
100 g (4 oz) desiccated coconut

Heat the oven to 150°C (300°F) mark 2. Dissolve the soda in the water. Melt the fat and syrup in a pan and then mix all the ingredients together to form a dough.

Roll the dough into small balls and place on greased baking sheets. Bake for about 20 minutes. Cool on a wire rack.

PEPPERMINT OAT BISCUITS

100 g (4 oz) lard
100 g (4 oz) margarine
2 tsp golden syrup
175 g (6 oz) sugar
¼ tsp bicarbonate of soda
4 tsp boiling water
225 g (8 oz) plain flour, sifted
225 g (8 oz) rolled oats
1 tsp baking powder
2 tsp vanilla essence

Filling
75 g (3 oz) butter
175 g (6 oz) icing sugar
a few drops of peppermint essence

Heat the oven to 200°C (400°F) mark 6. To make the biscuits: cream the lard, margarine, syrup and sugar until light and fluffy. Dissolve the soda in the boiling water and add to the creamed mixture together with all the other ingredients and work to form a dough. Roll out the dough on a lightly floured board and cut into rounds. Place on well greased baking sheets and bake for 15–20 minutes or until pale brown. Cool on a wire rack.

For the filling: cream the butter until it is soft. Gradually add the sifted icing sugar and cream together. Add the peppermint essence to taste and beat thoroughly.

When the biscuits are cold, sandwich together with the filling.

CHOCOLATE OAT BISCUITS

100 g (4 oz) self-raising flour
100 g (4 oz) rolled oats
75 g (3 oz) caster sugar
50 g (2 oz) lard
50 g (2 oz) margarine
1 tsp golden syrup
1 tsp bicarbonate of soda
1 tsp vanilla essence
1 tbsp boiling water

Filling
50 g (2 oz) butter
100 g (4 oz) icing sugar
1 tbsp cocoa powder

Topping
cooking chocolate (plain or milk)

Heat the oven to 180°C (350°F) mark 4. For the biscuits: mix the sifted flour, oats and sugar together in a bowl, then rub in the lard and margarine. Mix the remaining ingredients together and add to the dry ingredients to make a fairly soft dough. Knead the dough into a ball, wrap in cling film or foil, and chill for 30 minutes.

Roll the dough out on a floured board and cut into 6-cm (2-inch) rounds then place on greased baking sheets. Bake for about 20 minutes. Cool on a wire rack.

For the filling: cream the butter until it is soft. Add the sifted icing sugar and cream together. Add the cocoa and beat well.

Sandwich the biscuits together in pairs with the filling and coat the tops with melted chocolate.

BUFTON BISCUITS

150 g (5 oz) margarine
100 g (4 oz) granulated sugar
100 g (4 oz) self-raising flour
1 tsp baking powder
25 g (1 oz) semolina
100 g (4 oz) rolled oats
2 tbsp golden syrup
pinch of salt
1 tsp bicarbonate of soda
2 tsp milk

Filling
50 g (2 oz) butter
100 g (4 oz) icing sugar
1 tsp cocoa powder
1 tsp coffee essence

Heat the oven to 180°C (350°F) mark 4. For the biscuits: cream the margarine and sugar together until soft and creamy. Sift the flour and baking powder together and add with the semolina, oats, syrup and salt to the creamed mixture. Lastly, add the soda mixed with the milk. Mix to form a smooth dough.

Shape into small, rough balls and place on a greased baking sheet. Bake for 15–20 minutes until they are set. Cool on a wire rack.

To make the filling: cream the butter until it is soft. Gradually add the sifted icing sugar, and cream together. Add the cocoa powder and coffee essence and beat the mixture well. When the biscuits are cold, sandwich them together with this mocha butter cream.

ANZAC COOKIES

175 g (6 oz) butter
1 tsp golden syrup
1 tsp bicarbonate of soda
2 tbsp boiling water
100 g (4 oz) plain flour, sifted
100 g (4 oz) rolled oats
175 g (6 oz) caster sugar
100 g (4 oz) raisins, chopped

Heat the oven to 150°C (300°F) mark 2. Melt the butter and syrup in a pan. Dissolve the soda in the water and add this to the butter. Mix together the flour, oats, sugar and raisins in a bowl and pour in the liquid. Mix thoroughly to form a dough.

Place teaspoons of the mixture on greased baking sheets, allowing room for spreading. Bake for about 15 minutes. Remove the biscuits carefully and cool on a wire rack.

MELTING MOMENTS

Makes 24

100 g (4 oz) butter
100 g (4 oz) caster sugar
1 egg
175 g (6 oz) self-raising flour, sifted
pinch of salt
50 g (2 oz) rolled oats
12 glacé cherries

Heat the oven to 180°C (350°F) mark 4.
Beat the butter until it is soft and creamy.
Add the sugar, and cream until the mixture
is light and fluffy and drops easily from the
spoon. Beat in the egg with 25 g (1 oz) of
the flour. Fold in the remaining flour and
the salt, and mix to form a stiff dough.
  Divide the mixture into 24 pieces and,
with wet hands, roll each one into a ball.
Roll the balls in the oats and place on
greased baking sheets, allowing room to
spread. Flatten each one slightly and place
half a glacé cherry in the centre of each
biscuit. Bake for 20 minutes. Allow to set a
little on the baking sheets then remove to a
wire rack and leave until cold.

DATE SLICES

100 g (4 oz) stoned dates, chopped
100 g (4 oz) self-raising flour
100 g (4 oz) butter or margarine
100 g (4 oz) caster sugar
100 g (4 oz) rolled oats

Heat the oven to 180°C (350°F) mark 4.
Simmer the dates with sufficient water to
barely cover them until the mixture
resembles thick jam. More water may be
added or boiled off if necessary.
  Sift the flour, and rub in fat until the
mixture resembles breadcrumbs, then mix
in the sugar and oats and knead together.
Press half of this mixture into a greased
Swiss roll tin, spread the dates on top, and
cover with the remainder of the dough.
  Bake for about 20 minutes or until the
surface is evenly browned. Cut into fingers
while it is still hot, but leave in the tin until
cool and firm.

NUT BISCUITS

In this chapter, walnuts, peanuts, almonds and other nuts are used to flavour, decorate or add texture to a selection of biscuits. Many use nuts which are interchangeable, so you can vary the flavours and textures as you please.

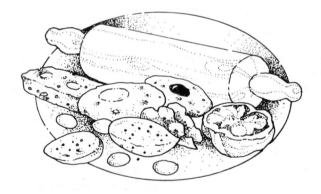

WALNUT BARS

225 g (8 oz) butter
225 g (8 oz) caster sugar
1 egg, separated
1 tsp vanilla essence
200 g (7 oz) plain flour, sifted
50 g (2 oz) shelled walnuts, chopped

Heat the oven to 180°C (350°F) mark 4.
Cream the butter and sugar together until light and fluffy. Beat in the egg yolk, vanilla essence and the flour. Press the mixture into a greased rectangular tin 25 x 18 x 5 cm (10 x 7 x 2 inches).

Lightly whisk the egg white and brush it over the dough. Sprinkle on the walnuts and bake for 45 minutes. Cool in the tin and cut into bars as it cools.

DATE STICKS

2 eggs
50 g (2 oz) caster sugar
pinch of salt
25 g (1 oz) butter, melted
450 g (1 lb) stoned dates, chopped
50 g (2 oz) shelled walnuts, chopped
175 g (6 oz) self-raising flour, sifted
1 tbsp hot water
caster sugar to sprinkle

Heat the oven to 190°C (375°F) mark 5.
Beat together the eggs, sugar, salt and melted butter. Mix in the dates and walnuts, then add the flour and hot water. Work to a dough.

Spread the mixture into two well greased and floured Swiss roll tins. Bake for 20–25 minutes. Cut into fingers and sprinkle with caster sugar whilst hot, then leave in the tins until cold before removing.

WALNUT CRISPS

225 g (8 oz) self-raising flour
75 g (3 oz) margarine
25 g (1 oz) butter
225 g (8 oz) soft brown sugar
100 g (4 oz) plain chocolate
100 g (4 oz) shelled walnuts,
    roughly chopped
1 egg, beaten

Heat the oven to 180°C (350°F) mark 4. Sift the flour into a bowl and rub in the margarine until the mixture resembles fine breadcrumbs. Mix in the sugar. Break the chocolate into small pieces and add to the dry ingredients together with the walnuts. Bind the mixture together with the egg.

Place small heaps of the dough on greased baking sheets and flatten with a fork. Bake for about 25 minutes. Cool on a wire rack.

COFFEE WALNUT BISCUITS

Makes about 20

100 g (4 oz) plain flour
2 tsp instant coffee powder
100 g (4 oz) butter
50 g (2 oz) caster sugar
50 g (2 oz) shelled walnuts, chopped

Heat the oven to 190°C (375°F) mark 5. Sift the flour and instant coffee together. Cream the butter and sugar together until light and fluffy, then add the rest of the ingredients. Place small teaspoons of the mixture on greased baking sheets leaving plenty of room for the biscuits to spread. Bake for 15–20 minutes. Cool on a wire rack.

PEANUT COOKIES

100 g (4 oz) soft margarine
100 g (4 oz) caster sugar
50 g (2 oz) salted peanuts
150 g (5 oz) self-raising flour

Heat the oven to 180°C (350°F) mark 4. Cream the margarine and sugar together until light and fluffy. Chop the nuts and stir in the mixture with the sifted flour to make a dough. Shape into walnut-sized balls and place on greased baking sheets. Bake for about 20 minutes. Cool on a wire rack.

ALMOND BUTTER CRISPS

Makes about 48

200 g (7 oz) butter or margarine
175 g (6 oz) caster sugar
1 tsp vanilla essence
1 tsp bicarbonate of soda
225 g (8 oz) self-raising flour
about 48 split almonds

Heat the oven to 180°C (350°F) mark 4. Work the butter into the sugar and when this has been absorbed, add the vanilla essence. Sift the soda with the flour and add to the other ingredients. Knead the dough until smooth.

Roll into balls the size of a walnut and place on lightly greased baking sheets leaving room for the biscuits to flatten and spread. Top each with a split almond. Bake for 15 minutes or until golden brown. Cool on a wire rack.

These light-as-air biscuits are often served in Denmark.

HAZELNUT BISCUITS

100 g (4 oz) butter
65 g (2½ oz) caster sugar
150 g (5 oz) plain flour, sifted
115 g (4½ oz) ground hazelnuts
a little honey
75 g (3 oz) plain block chocolate

Heat the oven to 180°C (350°F) mark 4. Cream together the butter and sugar until light and fluffy. Stir the flour and 75 g (3 oz) of the ground hazelnuts into the mixture. Knead into a ball and roll out thinly. Cut into rounds using a 5-cm (2½-inch) cutter. Place the rounds on a greased baking sheet and bake for 12 minutes. Cool on a wire rack.

When cool, sandwich the rounds together with honey. Melt the chocolate in a bowl over hot water. Roll the edges of the biscuits in the melted chocolate and then in the remainder of the ground hazelnuts.

NAPOLEON HATS

50 g (2 oz) butter
50 g (2 oz) caster sugar
½ egg
100 g (4 oz) plain flour
pinch of baking powder

Almond paste
50 g (2 oz) icing sugar
25 g (1 oz) ground almonds
a little egg

Icing
50 g (2 oz) icing sugar
2 tsp water

Heat the oven to 180°C (350°F) mark 4. To make the biscuits: cream the butter and sugar until light and fluffy. Beat in the egg and then mix to a stiff dough with the sifted flour and baking powder. Roll the dough out thinly and cut into rounds.

To make the almond paste: mix the icing sugar and ground almonds and add sufficient beaten egg to mix to a smooth consistency. Roll the almond paste into balls and place one on each biscuit. Fold up the two sides of the biscuits to make a shape like Napoleon's hat and place on greased baking sheets. Bake for about 20 minutes. Cool on a wire rack.

For the icing: mix the icing sugar with the water and beat until smooth. When the biscuits are cold, top each one with a little icing and leave to set.

CHERRY SNOWBALLS

Makes about 36

225 g (8 oz) butter
50 g (2 oz) icing sugar, sifted
225 g (8 oz) plain flour, sifted
pinch of salt
100 g (4 oz) shelled walnuts,
* chopped*
1 tsp vanilla essence
glacé cherries
caster sugar for coating

Heat the oven to 160°C (325°F) mark 3. Cream the butter with the icing sugar until light and fluffy. Add the rest of the ingredients except for the cherries to the creamed mixture and mix well.

Flatten teaspoons of the dough in the palms of your hands. Place a cherry on each round and cover it by pinching the dough up and around it. Roll into balls and place on a greased baking sheet.

Bake for 35 minutes. While still hot, roll the biscuits in caster sugar then cool on a wire rack.

ALMOND BARS

Makes about 30

225 g (8 oz) plain flour
150 g (6 oz) butter
100 g (4 oz) icing sugar, sifted
100 g (4 oz) blanched almonds, very
* finely chopped*
1 egg white
2 tsp coffee essence

Sift the flour on to a working surface and make a well in the centre. Cut the butter into pieces and put into the well with the sugar. Work the butter and sugar together with the fingertips, then gradually work in the flour. Finally work in the almonds and knead to a smooth dough. Wrap the dough in greaseproof paper and chill for 20–30 minutes.

Heat the oven to 190°C (375°F) mark 5. Grease two or three baking sheets. Using half the dough at a time, roll out to a rectangle about 5 mm (¼ inch) thick. Mark into a criss-cross pattern with a sharp knife. Mix the egg white and coffee essence together and brush all over the surface. Cut the dough into bars about 7.5 x 4 cm (3 x 1½ inches) and transfer carefully to the baking sheets. Repeat with the remaining dough.

Bake for about 15 minutes or until lightly coloured. Cool on a wire rack.

NUT AND FRUIT SHORTBREAD

175 g (6 oz) butter
75 g (3 oz) caster sugar
25 g (1 oz) ground rice
225 g (8 oz) plain flour
25 g (1 oz) glacé cherries, chopped
25 g (1 oz) angelica, chopped
50 g (2 oz) blanched almonds

Heat the oven to 180°C (350°F) mark 4.
Cream the butter and sugar until light and fluffy. Add the ground rice and sifted flour. Stir in the cherries, angelica and half the almonds and work to form a dough.

Place the dough in a greased 23-cm (9-inch) square cake tin and press the remainder of the almonds on the top. Bake for 30–40 minutes. Cool in the tin, marking into fingers when just firm.

CHOCOLATE NUT BISCUITS

Makes about 50

100 g (4 oz) butter
175 g (6 oz) caster sugar
1 egg, beaten
40 g (1½ oz) plain chocolate, grated
225 g (8 oz) plain flour, sifted
½ tsp cream of tartar
½ tsp bicarbonate of soda
pinch of salt
a few drops of vanilla essence
40 g (1½ oz) shelled walnuts,
    chopped

Cream the butter until soft. Add the sugar and continue until light and fluffy. Add the egg, then the chocolate, together with all the other ingredients. Form the dough into a roll about 4 cm (1½ inches) in diameter, wrap in cling film or foil and chill until firm. Heat the oven to 180°C (350°F) mark 4.

Slice the roll thinly with a sharp knife. Place the rounds on greased baking sheets leaving room to spread. Bake for 10 minutes. Cool on a wire rack.

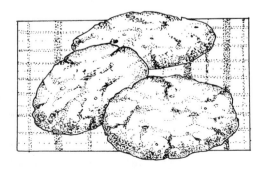

LACE BISCUITS

100 g (4 oz) margarine
100 g (4 oz) caster sugar
juice of 1 lemon
100 g (4 oz) chopped almonds
50 g (2 oz) plain flour
pinch of salt

Heat the oven to 180°C (350°F) mark 4.
Cream the margarine, sugar and lemon juice until light and fluffy. Add the almonds and then stir in the sifted flour and salt. Mix well to form a dough.

Break off pieces of dough the size of a walnut and place on greased baking sheets leaving room for the biscuits to spread. Press with a fork and bake for 15–20 minutes. Do not remove from the baking sheets until they are cold. Store in an airtight container.

FRUITY BRITTLES

100 g (4 oz) self-raising flour
pinch of salt
150 g (5 oz) butter or margarine
100 g (4 oz) caster sugar
100 g (4 oz) mixed dried fruit,
  chopped
50 g (2 oz) shelled walnuts, chopped
1 egg
100 g (4 oz) cornflakes, crushed

Heat the oven to 200°C (400°F) mark 6. Sift the flour and salt into a bowl and rub in the butter until the mixture resembles breadcrumbs. Mix in the sugar, fruit and nuts. Beat the egg and work into the mixture.

Roll ping-pong ball sized pieces of the mixture in the crushed cornflakes. Place on greased baking sheets, leaving room for them to spread. Bake for 10–15 minutes. Cool on a wire rack.

CRESCENT BISCUITS

200 g (7 oz) plain flour
75 g (3 oz) butter
75 g (3 oz) margarine
50 g (2 oz) caster sugar
75 g (3 oz) ground almonds
a few drops of vanilla essence
caster sugar for sprinkling

Heat the oven to 150°C (300°F) mark 2. Sift the flour into a bowl and rub in the fats until the mixture resembles breadcrumbs. Add the sugar, almonds and essence and knead the mixture to form a stiff paste.

Roll the dough out on a floured board to a thickness of 1 cm (½ inch). Cut into crescent shapes using either a plain or a fluted cutter, and place on greased baking sheets. Bake for 30 minutes. Sprinkle with caster sugar and cool on a wire rack.

CRESTON DROPS

100 g (4 oz) butter
50 g (2 oz) caster sugar
2 eggs
3 squares chocolate, melted
100 g (4 oz) shelled walnuts,
    chopped
100 g (4 oz) raisins
225 g (8 oz) plain flour
1 tsp salt
½ tsp bicarbonate of soda
6 tbsp milk

Heat the oven to 200°C (400°F) mark 6. Cream the butter and sugar together until light and fluffy. Beat in the eggs, then the melted chocolate, nuts and raisins. Sift the flour with the salt and soda and add them to the mixture alternating with the milk.

Drop teaspoons of the mixture on to greased baking sheets and flatten with a spoon. Bake for 10–15 minutes. Cool on a wire rack.

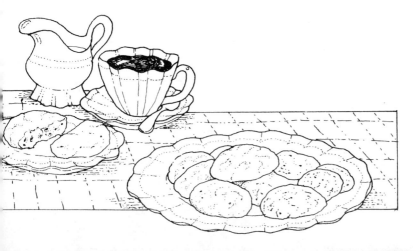

KING HAAKON BISCUITS

100 g (4 oz) icing sugar
pinch of salt
225 g (8 oz) plain flour
225 g (8 oz) butter
50 g (2 oz) shelled walnuts, chopped
50 g (2 oz) glacé cherries

Heat the oven to 150°C (300°F) mark 2. Sift the icing sugar, salt and flour together and rub in the butter until the mixture resembles breadcrumbs. Add the other ingredients and form the dough into a good-shaped roll. Wrap in foil and put in the refrigerator until firm.

When the dough is very firm, cut into thin slices. Place on greased baking sheets and bake for 20–25 minutes. Cool on a wire rack.

CARDAMOM COOKIES

Makes 30

75 g (3 oz) icing sugar
225 g (8 oz) plain flour
225 g (8 oz) butter, softened
50 g (2 oz) shelled walnuts, chopped
1 tsp almond essence
½ tsp ground cardamom
pinch of salt
icing sugar to dredge

Heat the oven to 180°C (350°F) mark 4. Sift the icing sugar and flour. Add the rest of the ingredients and work to give a firm mixture. Shape the dough into 2.5-cm (1-inch) balls and place 5 cm (2 inches) apart on greased baking sheets. Bake for 20 minutes or until golden brown. Cool on a wire rack. Dredge the cookies with icing sugar before serving.

MARZIPAN BISCUITS

100 g (4 oz) caster sugar
75 g (3 oz) ground almonds
finely grated rind of 1 small orange
2 small egg yolks
a few drops of almond essence
25 g (1 oz) flaked almonds

Heat the oven to 190°C (375°F) mark 5. Mix the caster sugar, ground almonds and orange rind together in a medium-sized mixing bowl. Make a well in the centre of the mixture and add the egg yolks and almond essence. Using a small spatula or your fingers, gradually work in the dry ingredients. Knead the mixture lightly until it forms a smooth dough. Shape into a ball, wrap in greaseproof paper or foil and chill for 10 minutes.

Sprinkle a board and rolling pin with icing sugar and roll the dough out very thinly. Using a 5-cm (2-inch) pastry cutter, cut the dough into rounds.

Place on greased baking sheets, spaced slightly apart. Put a few almonds on each round. Bake in the centre of the oven for 8–10 minutes or until golden brown. Cool on a wire rack.

VANILLA KIPFERL

Makes about 48

225 g (8 oz) butter
225 g (8 oz) plain flour, sifted
pinch of salt
1 tsp vanilla essence
100 g (4 oz) ground almonds or
    hazelnuts or a mixture of both
100 g (4 oz) caster sugar
sifted icing sugar or caster sugar for
    coating

Work the butter into the flour, salt, vanilla essence, nuts and caster sugar until a dough is formed. Chill for 1 hour.

Heat the oven to 160°C (325°F) mark 3. Pinch off pieces of dough the size of a walnut and roll into 'pencils' about 2 cm (¾ inch) thick and 6 cm (2½ inches) long, then bend into crescent shapes. When forming the biscuits, try not to use any flour as this will toughen them; they may be rolled on non-stick parchment.

Arrange the crescents on ungreased baking sheets, leaving about 2.5 cm (1 inch) between each biscuit, to allow them room to spread. Bake for 20 minutes or until a pale golden colour. Leave for 3 minutes to firm up and then remove them from the baking sheets and dip in a bowl of icing or caster sugar.

62

ALMOND BISCUITS

Makes about 18

225 g (8 oz) soft margarine
100 g (4 oz) caster sugar
50 g (2 oz) ground almonds
150 g (6 oz) self-raising flour, sifted
a few drops almond essence
50 g (2 oz) sultanas
40–50 g (1½–2 oz) flaked almonds

Glaze
3 tbsp apricot jam
1 tbsp water

Grease an oblong tin about 28 x 18 x 4 cm (11 x 7 x 1½ inches) Heat the oven to 160°C (325°F) mark 3. Cream the fat and sugar together until light and fluffy. Work in the almonds, flour, a few drops of almond essence and the sultanas.

Put into the tin and spread out evenly, making sure the corners are well filled. Sprinkle with the flaked almonds and press in gently. Bake for 50–60 minutes or until lightly browned and just firm.

Heat the apricot jam and water together in a saucepan until melted, then boil for 1 minute. Rub through a sieve and brush over the almonds whilst still warm. Leave in the tin until cold then cut into squares.

MA' MOULE

75 g (3 oz) semolina
25 g (1 oz) plain flour
75 g (3 oz) butter
2 tsp boiling water
40 g (1½ oz) shelled walnuts, finely chopped
40 g (1½ oz) caster sugar
½ tsp rose flower water
½ tsp orange flower water
caster sugar for sprinkling

Make a dough from the semolina, flour, butter, and boiling water by kneading together. Knead lightly, cover and leave overnight.

The next day, heat the oven to 190°C (375°F) mark 5. Roll the dough into small balls. Make a small hollow in the centre of each one with your fingertip. Blend the walnuts, sugar, rose and orange flower water and use to fill the hollows. Pinch the edges together to cover the filling and then flatten the biscuits with the palm of your hand. Place on greased baking sheets and bake for 10–15 minutes until they are golden brown. While they are still hot, sprinkle them with fine sugar. Cool on a wire rack.

PETITS FOURS

1 egg
50 g (2 oz) ground almonds
50 g (2 oz) caster sugar
rice paper
angelica to decorate
glacé cherries to decorate

Beat the egg, then mix it to a paste with the almonds and sugar. Place the mixture in a forcing bag fitted with a large star nozzle and pipe small shapes on to baking sheets lined with rice paper. Allow to stand for 24 hours.

Heat the oven to 180°C (350°F) mark 4. Decorate the biscuits with pieces of angelica and halved or quartered cherries and bake for 15–20 minutes or until light brown. Cool on the trays and, when cold, tear apart, removing excess rice paper.

There are many variations on this recipe, and the biscuits can be decorated in many different ways.

STRAWBERRY DELIGHTS

5 tbsp butter or margarine
225 g (8 oz) dates
2 eggs
pinch of salt
1 tsp vanilla essence
100 g (4 oz) rice crispies
75 g (3 oz) chopped nuts
75 g (3 oz) desiccated coconut
100 g (4 oz) granulated sugar
a few drops of red food colouring
angelica or green marzipan

Melt the butter in a pan, add the chopped dates and cook over a low heat. When the mixture begins to thicken, add the beaten eggs, salt and vanilla. Allow the mixture to cool a little, then add the rice crispies, nuts and coconut. Turn the mixture on to a large plate and leave to cool.

Make the sugar red by tinting it with the red food colouring. Take small pieces of the mixture and shape them into 'strawberries'. Roll in red sugar. Top each one with a leaf of green angelica or marzipan.

This recipe is excellent for freezing.

BUTTER KNOTS

Makes about 16

100 g (4 oz) butter
50 g (2 oz) caster sugar
1 egg, lightly beaten
50 g (2 oz) ground almonds
150 g (6 oz) plain flour, sifted
flaked almonds
50 g (2 oz) icing sugar, sifted
a little lemon juice or water to mix

Grease several baking sheets which will fit into the refrigerator.

Cream the butter and sugar together until light and fluffy then beat in about three-quarters of the egg. Add the ground almonds and flour and work together to form a dough.

Take about half of the mixture, break off small pieces, roll into strips with the hands and then form into fancy knot shapes on the baking sheets. Chill in the refrigerator for at least 30 minutes. Heat the oven to 220°C (425°F) mark 7.

Meanwhile shape the rest of the dough in the same way then brush with the remainder of the egg and sprinkle with the nuts. Chill.

Bake both varieties of knots for 10–15 minutes. Make up the glacé icing and use to brush over the plain knots as soon as they come out of the oven. Remove all to a wire rack and leave to cool and set.

ALMOND COCOROONS

Makes about 24

2 egg whites
75 g (3 oz) desiccated coconut
40 g (1½ oz) ground almonds
100 g (4 oz) caster sugar
rice paper

Heat the oven to 160°C (325°F) mark 3. Whisk the egg whites until stiff. Mix the coconut, ground almonds and sugar together and fold lightly into the beaten egg whites.

Place the mixture in small rounds (about 2 teaspoons at a time) on baking sheets lined with rice paper. Bake for 20–25 minutes then cool on a wire rack and pull apart, removing surplus rice paper when cold.

ALMOND JUMBLES

Makes 16–20

100 g (4 oz) butter or margarine
100 g (4 oz) caster sugar
1 egg, beaten
almond essence
150 g (6 oz) plain flour, sifted
50 g (2 oz) ground almonds

Grease two baking sheets. Heat the oven to 180°C (350°F) mark 4. Cream the fat and sugar together until light and fluffy. Beat in the egg and a few drops of almond essence. Gradually work in the flour and the ground almonds to give a firm but pliable dough, and knead lightly.

Divide the dough into two pieces and roll each into a long sausage 1–2 cm (½–¾ inch) in diameter. Cut into 10-cm (4-inch) lengths and put on to the baking sheets in 'S' shapes. Bake for 15–20 minutes or until a pale golden brown. Cool on a wire rack.

ALMOND BALLS

Makes about 24

100 g (4 oz) butter or margarine
100 g (4 oz) caster sugar
100 g (4 oz) ground almonds
1 egg, separated
1 tsp vanilla essence
100 g (4 oz) plain flour, sifted
slivers of almonds

Heat the oven to 180°C (350°F) mark 4. Cream the butter and sugar together until light and fluffy. Stir in the ground almonds, the egg yolk, vanilla essence and the flour. Knead the dough until it is well blended.

Roll into small balls about 2.5 cm (1 inch) in diameter. Place on a lightly greased baking sheet and press a slivered almond on top of each one. Brush with the slightly beaten egg white and bake for 20–30 minutes. Cool on a wire rack. When cold, store in an airtight container.

HAZELNUT CRUNCHIES

Makes about 12 pairs

100 g (4 oz) hazelnuts, toasted
100 g (4 oz) butter
65 g (2½ oz) caster sugar
125 g (5 oz) plain flour
2 tbsp thick honey
100 g (4 oz) icing sugar, sifted
2 tsp coffee essence
1 tbsp water

Grease two or three baking sheets. Heat the oven to 180°C (350°F) mark 4.

Reserve 36 nuts and grind the remainder finely in a mouli grater or blender. Cream the butter and sugar together until light and fluffy. Gradually work in the ground nuts and flour. Cover and chill for about 15 minutes.

Roll the dough out on a floured board to about 3 mm (⅛ inch) thick and cut into 7-cm (2½-inch) rounds using a plain cutter. Lift carefully on to the baking sheets and cook in the centre of the oven for about 10–15 minutes or until lightly coloured. Cool on a wire rack.

For the icing: mix the icing sugar with the coffee essence and sufficient water to give a thick coating consistency. Sandwich the biscuits in pairs with the honey then put a dab of icing on top of each one. Add 3 hazelnuts to each dab of icing and leave to set.

ORANGE CARAMEL ROLLS

Makes about 16

75 g (3 oz) butter
100 g (4 oz) caster sugar
50 g (2 oz) plain flour
25 g (1 oz) cornflour
grated rind and juice of 1 orange
100 g (4 oz) flaked almonds

Line baking sheets with non-stick parchment. Greese the handles of several wooden spoons. Heat the oven to 180°C (350°F) mark 4. Cream the butter and sugar until light and fluffy. Sift the flour and cornflour together and add to the creamed mixture alternating with the orange rind and juice. Mix in the flaked almonds.

Drop teaspoons of the mixture on to the prepared baking sheets keeping well apart. Bake for about 25 minutes.

Cool on the baking sheets for a few minutes then remove carefully and wind round the wooden spoon handles. Cool on wire racks until firm then slip off and leave on the racks until cold. Store in an airtight container.

MACAROONIES

Makes about 18

75 g (3 oz) plain flour
25 g (1 oz) ground rice
25 g (1 oz) caster sugar
50 g (2 oz) butter
1 egg yolk

Topping
1 egg white
75 g (3 oz) caster sugar
50 g (2 oz) ground almonds
a few drops almond essence

a little apricot jam

Grease two or three baking sheets. Heat the oven to 180°C (350°F) mark 4. Put the flour, rice and sugar in a bowl. Gradually work in the softened butter and the egg yolk and knead lightly together. Roll out on a lightly floured board to about 3 mm (⅛ inch) thick. With a fluted 5-cm (2-inch) cutter, stamp out as many rounds as possible.

Place on the baking sheets. For the topping: whisk the egg white until stiff; fold in the sugar, almonds and almond essence. Place the mixture in a piping bag fitted with a small plain nozzle and pipe a ring around the edge of each biscuit.

Bake for 15–20 minutes until a light brown. Cool on a wire rack and store in an airtight container. Before serving, fill the centre of each biscuit with apricot jam.

TRADITIONAL AND FOREIGN BISCUITS

This chapter contains a range of well known favourites such as florentines, tuiles, Easter biscuits and Garibaldis, mixed with a selection of foreign biscuits which include Viennese, Belgian, Finnish and German varieties.

MACAROONS

2 egg whites
100 g (4 oz) ground almonds
25 g (1 oz) ground rice
225 g (8 oz) caster sugar
rice paper
a few split almonds
egg white for glazing

Heat the oven to 180°C (350°F) mark 4.
Whisk the egg whites until stiff, then fold in
the ground almonds, ground rice and sugar.
Line baking sheets with rice paper. Place
small heaps of the mixture on the rice
paper, spaced out so that there is room for
them to spread. Top each one with a split
almond and glaze with egg white. Bake for
25–30 minutes. Cool on the baking sheets
then break up, tearing off excess rice paper.

CORNISH GINGER FAIRINGS

100 g (4 oz) butter
100 g (4 oz) caster sugar
1 tbsp golden syrup
175 g (6 oz) self-raising flour
1 tsp ground ginger
pinch of bicarbonate of soda

Heat the oven to 200°C (400°F) mark 6.
Melt the butter, sugar and syrup in a pan.
Sift the dry ingredients into a bowl and add
the melted mixture, stirring to form a
dough. Roll the dough into small balls and
place on greased baking sheets. Bake for
10–15 minutes or until golden brown. Cool
on a wire rack.

APPLEBY FAIRINGS

450 g (1 lb) plain flour
275 g (10 oz) butter
225 g (8 oz) caster sugar
pinch of salt
1 egg yolk

Heat the oven to 180–190°C (350–375°F)
mark 4–5. Sift the flour into a bowl and rub
in the butter until the mixture resembles
fine breadcrumbs, then add the sugar and
salt. Drop in the egg yolk and work the
mixture into a dry dough.
   Roll out on a lightly floured board to a
thickness of 5 mm (¼ inch) and cut into
small rounds. Place on greased baking
sheets and impress the biscuits with a
pattern or prick them all over. Bake for
about 35–40 minutes. Cool on a wire rack.

KOURABIÉDES

Makes about 40

225 g (8 oz) butter
75 g (3 oz) caster sugar
2 tbsp ouzo
¼ tsp vanilla essence
1 egg yolk
275 g (10 oz) plain flour
½ tsp baking powder
40 whole cloves
icing sugar for sprinkling
rose water

Heat the oven to 190°C (375°F) mark 5. Cream the butter and sugar until light and fluffy. Beat in the ouzo, vanilla essence and egg yolk. Sift the flour and baking powder and add to the mixture. Mix well to make a firm dough.

Roll rounded teaspoons of the dough into balls and place on baking sheets lined with non-stick baking parchment. Flatten slightly and spike each cookie with a clove. Bake for 20 minutes.

Transfer the cookies immediately to a wire rack and, while they are still hot, sprinkle with icing sugar and rose water. Leave until cold.

FLORENTINES

150 ml (¼ pint) single cream
75 g (3 oz) caster sugar
75 g (3 oz) glacé cherries, mixed
    peel and raisins, mixed
100 g (4 oz) flaked almonds
2 tsp butter
1 scant tbsp self-raising flour

Topping
175 g (6 oz) block plain chocolate

Heat the oven to 190°C (375°F) mark 5. Heat the cream and sugar slowly in a thick saucepan until the sugar has dissolved. Bring to the boil, then tip in the chopped fruit, nuts, butter and flour. Remove from the heat and mix thoroughly with a wooden spoon.

Line a baking sheet with non-stick baking parchment. Place small teaspoons of the mixture 15 cm (6 inches) apart on the baking sheet. Bake for about 10 minutes, or until evenly browned. Remove the biscuits at once from the sheet and cool them on a wire rack.

For the topping: melt the chocolate in a basin over hot water. When the biscuits are cold, spread their undersides with melted chocolate and mark the chocolate with a fork. Leave the biscuits upside down on a flat surface to dry.

GARIBALDI BISCUITS

200 g (7 oz) self-raising flour
25 g (1 oz) cornflour
50 g (2 oz) caster sugar
pinch of salt
50 g (2 oz) butter or margarine
1 egg yolk
a little milk
75–100 g (3–4 oz) currants
caster sugar for sprinkling

Heat the oven to 200°C (400°F) mark 6. Sift the flour, cornflour, sugar and salt into a bowl. Rub in the butter until the mixture resembles breadcrumbs. Mix to a stiffish dough with the egg yolk and milk.

Turn on to a floured board and roll the dough out to a thin oblong. Trim the edges then sprinkle one half of the dough with the currants. Fold over the other half of the dough and press the edges well together.

Roll the dough out lightly with a floured rolling pin until it is about 2.5 mm (⅛ inch) thick. Cut into 5-cm (2-inch) squares. Place on greased baking sheets and bake for 15 minutes or until golden brown. Sprinkle with caster sugar and cool on a wire rack.

LANCASHIRE NUTS

100 g (4 oz) butter
100 g (4 oz) caster sugar
1 egg
100 g (4 oz) plain flour
100 g (4 oz) cornflour
1 tbsp baking powder

Filling
50 g (2 oz) butter
100 g (4 oz) icing sugar
a few drops of vanilla essence

Heat the oven to 180°C (350°F) mark 4. For the biscuits: cream the butter and sugar until light and fluffy. Add the egg and beat together. Sift together the flour, cornflour and baking powder, add to the mixture and work to form a paste. Place teaspoons of the dough on a greased baking sheet and bake for 8–10 minutes until golden brown.

To make the filling: cream the butter until it is soft. Gradually add the sifted icing sugar and cream together. Add the vanilla essence and beat the mixture well.

When they are cold, sandwich the biscuits together in pairs with the filling.

DANISH SPECIER BISCUITS

Makes 40

225 g (8 oz) plain flour
75 g (3 oz) icing sugar
175 g (6 oz) butter or margarine
25 g (1 oz) blanched almonds,
    chopped
granulated sugar to coat

Sift the flour and icing sugar into a bowl and rub in the fat. Stir in the almonds and mix to form a dough. Shape the dough into two 'sausages' about 5 cm (2 inches) thick and roll in granulated sugar until they are completely covered. Wrap in cling film or foil and chill until firm.

Heat the oven to 200°C (400°F) mark 6. Cut the dough into 5-mm (¼-inch) thick slices and place on ungreased baking sheets. Bake for 8–10 minutes until light brown around the edges. Cool on a wire rack.

GRASMERE GINGERBREAD

Makes about 18

450 g (1 lb) plain flour
2 tsp ground ginger
1 tsp bicarbonate of soda
1 tsp cream of tartar
225 g (8 oz) soft brown sugar
225 g (8 oz) butter or margarine

Heat the oven to 150°C (300°F) mark 2. Sift the flour, ginger, soda and cream of tartar into a bowl, stir in the sugar and then rub in the fat until the mixture resembles fine breadcrumbs. Press the mixture into a greased tin 25 x 30 cm (10 x 12 inches) lined with greased greaseproof paper. Bake for about 30 minutes. Allow the gingerbread to cool slightly before cutting into pieces. Remove from the tin when cold.

GRANTHAM GINGER DROPS

Makes about 24

100 g (4 oz) butter or margarine
100 g (4 oz) caster sugar
100 g (4 oz) self-raising flour
2 tsp ground ginger

Heat the oven to 125°C (250°F) mark ½. Lightly cream the fat and sugar together until soft, but do not cream too much. Sift the flour and ginger together and work into the mixture to form a stiff dough.

Roll the dough into small balls and place on ungreased baking sheets. Bake for 30–40 minutes. Cool on a wire rack.

EASTER BISCUITS

75 g (3 oz) butter
75 g (3 oz) caster sugar
1 egg yolk
pinch of mixed spice
50 g (2 oz) currants
15 g (½ oz) mixed peel
175 g (6 oz) plain flour, sifted
a little milk

Glaze
1 egg white
caster sugar

Heat the oven to 180°C (350°F) mark 4. Soften the butter, add the sugar, and cream the mixture until light and fluffy. Add the egg yolk, spice, peel and flour and mix to a stiff dough with the milk. Roll the dough out thinly on a floured board and cut into rounds about 7.5 cm (3 inches) in diameter, using a plain or fluted cutter. Place on greased baking sheets and bake for 15–20 minutes. After 10 minutes, brush with the egg white and sprinkle with caster sugar, then return to the oven until a light golden brown. Cool on a wire rack.

74

BELGIAN SUGAR BISCUITS

75 g (3 oz) butter
150 g (5 oz) caster sugar
1 egg yolk
175 g (6 oz) plain flour
1 tsp ground ginger

Cream the butter and sugar until light and fluffy, then add the egg yolk. Add the sifted flour and ginger, and mix thoroughly. Shape the dough into a 5-cm (2-inch) diameter roll, wrap and leave in the refrigerator until firm.

Heat the oven to 160°C (325°F) mark 3. Using a sharp knife, cut the roll into thin slices approximately 5 mm (¼ inch) thick. Place on greased baking sheets and bake for about 15–20 minutes until the biscuits are lightly browned. Cool on a wire rack.

VIENNESE BISCUITS

100 g (4 oz) butter or margarine
25 g (1 oz) icing sugar
a few drops of vanilla essence
100 g (4 oz) plain flour, sifted
glacé cherries

Heat the oven to 180°C (350°F) mark 4. Cream the butter and sugar until light and fluffy, stir in the essence and gradually work in the flour.

Put the mixture in a forcing bag fitted with a large star nozzle and pipe fingers, rounds, or other shapes on to greased baking sheets. Decorate each with a cherry or piece of cherry. Bake for 15–20 minutes. Leave to cool before removing from the baking sheet. Store in an airtight container.

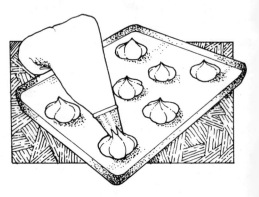

FINNISH SHORTBREAD

350 g (12 oz) plain flour
225 g (8 oz) butter
100 g (4 oz) caster sugar
1 egg yolk

Coating
2–3 egg yolks
chopped almonds
granulated sugar

Heat the oven to 180°C (350°F) mark 4. Sift the flour into a bowl and rub in the butter until the mixture resembles fine breadcrumbs. Add the egg yolk and work to form a dough and knead lightly. Roll the dough into long 'sausages' the thickness of your little finger and cut into 1-cm (½-inch) lengths.

Dip the pieces of dough in the beaten egg yolks, then roll in a mixture of chopped almonds and sugar. Place on greased baking sheets and bake for 20 minutes until golden brown. Cool on a wire rack.

JUMBLES

225 g (8 oz) plain flour
175 g (6 oz) butter
225 g (8 oz) caster sugar
finely grated rind of 1 lemon
1 egg (size 1 or 2), beaten
caster sugar for dredging

Heat the oven to 180°C (350°F) mark 4. Sift the flour into a bowl and rub in the butter until the mixture resembles breadcrumbs. Add the sugar and the lemon rind and then stir in the beaten egg and work to form into a smooth dough.

Roll the dough into long thin 'sausages'. Cut them into 10-cm (4-inch) lengths and make them into wheel or 'S' shapes. Place on greased baking sheets and bake for 15–20 minutes or until evenly browned. Dredge with caster sugar immediately and cool on a wire rack.

BRANDY CORNETS

Makes 12–16

50 g (2 oz) butter or blended white
  vegetable fat
50 g (2 oz) golden syrup
50 g (2 oz) caster sugar
50 g (2 oz) plain flour
a large pinch of ground ginger

Line two baking sheets with non-stick parchment. Grease the outer surface of several cream horn tins. Heat the oven to 160°C (325°F) mark 3.

Melt the fat in a saucepan with the syrup and sugar, then remove from the heat. Sift the flour with the ginger and stir into the melted mixture.

Put teaspoons of the mixture well apart on the baking sheets and cook for 8–10 minutes or until golden brown. Cool until just firm enough to remove with a palette knife then wind quickly round the cream horn tins. Cool on a wire rack until firm then slip off the tins. Repeat with the remaining mixture. Serve as they are or fill with whipped cream.

BOURBON BISCUITS

100 g (4 oz) plain flour
15 g (½ oz) cocoa
½ tsp baking powder
50 g (2 oz) butter
50 g (2 oz) caster sugar
1 tbsp golden syrup
granulated sugar to coat

Filling
25 g (1 oz) plain chocolate
1½ tbsp water
50 g (2 oz) icing sugar, sifted
a few drops of vanilla essence

Heat the oven to 160°C (325°F) mark 3. To make the biscuits: sift together the flour, cocoa and baking powder. Cream the butter and caster sugar until light and fluffy then beat in the syrup and stir in half the flour mixture. Turn the dough on to a lightly floured board and knead in the remaining flour mixture. Roll the dough out to a thickness of 5 mm (¼ inch), sprinkle with granulated sugar and press the sugar in with a rolling pin. Cut into neat fingers and place on a greased baking sheet. Bake for 15–20 minutes. Cool on a wire rack.

For the filling: melt the chocolate in the water, add the icing sugar and essence, and beat together until smooth. When the biscuits are cool, sandwich together with the filling.

GERMAN BISCUITS

200 g (7 oz) plain flour
½ tsp baking powder
½ tsp ground cinnamon
100 g (4 oz) butter or margarine
100 g (4 oz) caster sugar
1 egg, beaten

Filling
raspberry jam

Icing
150 g (6 oz) icing sugar
1½ tbsp water

glacé cherries to decorate

Heat the oven to 180°C (350°F) mark 4. For the biscuits: sift the flour, baking powder and cinnamon into a bowl, then rub in the fat until the mixture resembles fine breadcrumbs. Add the sugar and mix to a stiff dough with the egg.

Roll the dough out to a thickness of 2.5 mm (⅛ inch) and cut into rounds about 5 cm (2 inches) in diameter. Place on greased baking sheets and bake for 10–15 minutes.

When the biscuits are cold, sandwich together with the jam. To make the icing: mix the sifted icing sugar with the water and beat until smooth. Ice the tops of the biscuits, then decorate with halved or quartered glacé cherries.

These biscuits taste even better if made the day before they are eaten.

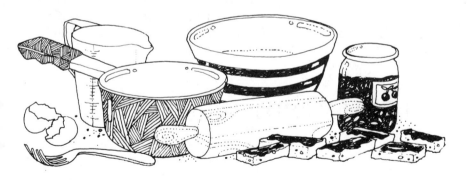

SHREWSBURY BISCUITS

100 g (4 oz) butter
100 g (4 oz) caster sugar
1 egg
grated rind and juice of ½ lemon
25 g (1 oz) currants
225 g (8 oz) plain flour
pinch of bicarbonate of soda

Cream the butter and sugar until light and fluffy, then beat in the egg, lemon rind and juice and the currants. Sift the flour and soda and work into the mixture. Knead well, cover and leave in the refrigerator overnight. Heat the oven to 180°C (350°F) mark 4. Roll the dough out to a thickness of 5 mm (¼ inch) and cut into rounds approx 6 cm (2½ inches) in diameter. Place on greased baking sheets and bake for about 20 minutes. Cool on a wire rack.

SHORTBREAD BISCUITS

150 g (6 oz) plain flour
100 g (4 oz) butter
50 g (2 oz) caster sugar
caster sugar for dredging

Sift the flour into a bowl, add the other ingredients and knead until the mixture has a soft consistency. Roll out on a floured board and cut into fingers. Place on lightly greased baking sheets and leave overnight. Heat the oven to 200°C (400°F) mark 6. Bake for 10–12 minutes or until golden brown. Dredge with caster sugar and cool on a wire rack.

GERMAN ALMOND BISCUITS

225 g (8 oz) butter
175 g (6 oz) caster sugar
1 egg
100 g (4 oz) self-raising flour
100 g (4 oz) plain flour
raspberry jam
1 tsp sugar for glazing
flaked almonds

Heat the oven to 150°C (300°F) mark 2. Cream the butter and sugar until light and fluffy and then add the beaten egg (keeping back a small quantity for glazing). Sift in the flours and mix well.

Divide the mixture in half and use one portion to cover the base of a well greased cake tin 18 cm (7 inches) in diameter. Spread this with raspberry jam then cover the jam with the remaining mixture.

Add a teaspoon of sugar to the remainder of the egg and use to glaze the dough, then sprinkle with flaked almonds. Bake for 45 minutes. Leave in the tin until almost cold, then cut into slices. Remove from the tin when quite cold.

This is equally good if the jam is omitted, but the mixture should then be spread over a larger tin.

TUILES

50 g (2 oz) butter
50 g (2 oz) caster sugar
2 egg whites
50 g (2 oz) plain flour
pinch of salt
grated rind of ½ lemon or
    a few drops of vanilla essence

Heat the oven to 190°C (375°F) mark 5. Soften the butter in a bowl over hot water but do not let it get oily. Beat lightly with a fork, gradually adding the sugar, until very light and fluffy. Beat in the unwhisked egg whites a little at a time.

Sift the flour with the salt into a bowl and fold into the mixture gently. Flavour with lemon rind or vanilla essence. Put into a forcing bag fitted with a 1-cm (½-inch) nozzle and pipe 5-cm (2-inch) lengths on to baking sheets lined with non-stick parchment, allowing room for the biscuits to spread. Bake for 10 minutes until golden brown around the edges.

While the Tuiles are still warm, remove from the baking sheets carefully and lay over a greased rolling pin to make them curl. Leave until cold.

These biscuits are usually served with a rich party dessert, special poached fruit or fresh soft drinks.

KICHELECH

225 g (8 oz) hard margarine or
  100 g (4 oz) butter and 100 g
  (4 oz) margarine
450 g (1 lb) self-raising flour
175 g (6 oz) caster sugar
2 tsp ground almonds
1 egg
milk or white wine to make a pliable
  dough

Heat the oven to 180°C (350°F) mark 4. Rub the margarine into the flour using fingertips. Add the sugar and ground almonds and mix to a pliable dough with the beaten egg and milk or white wine. Roll out thinly and then cut into rounds using a plain cutter. Moisten and sprinkle with sugar. Place on greased trays and cook until light brown – about 15 minutes.

QUICK KICHELECH

Makes 36

2 large eggs
150 ml (¼ pint) cooking oil
2 tsp vanilla essence
1 tsp grated lemon rind
150–175 g (5–6 oz) caster sugar
225 g (8 oz) self raising flour
sugar and chopped nuts for
  decoration

Heat the oven to 200°C (400°F) mark 6. Beat the eggs until well blended. Stir in the oil, vanilla and lemon rind. Beat in the sugar until the mixture thickens, then stir in the flour, making a soft, thick batter.

Drop the batter from a teaspoon on to a greased baking tin, leaving 5 cm (2 inch) between the biscuits. Dip the bottom of a tumbler in oil and then in granulated sugar and use to flatten each biscuit gently.

Sprinkle with chopped nuts or dessicated coconut. Cook for 10 minutes or until golden brown.

This Jewish recipe makes a very economical batch of biscuits.

PASSOVER MERINGUES

2 egg whites
175 g (6 oz) caster or icing sugar
100 g (4 oz) raisins
50 g (2 oz) chopped nuts

Heat the oven to 150°C (300°F) mark 2.

Beat the egg whites until stiff. Add the sugar a spoonful at a time and beat until stiff after each addition. Carefully fold in the raisins and nuts. Place in small heaps on a greased baking tray or a baking tray lined with non-stick parchment. Cook for about 30 minutes, until crisp.

For the week of Passover, the Jewish festival celebrating the Exodus from Egypt, no flour is eaten. This recipe is one of the many delicious ways round the problem of baking without flour.

DUTCH JANHAGEL

100 g (4 oz) unsalted butter
150 g (6 oz) plain flour
75 g (3 oz) caster sugar
½ tsp ground cinnamon
25 g (1 oz) flaked almonds
a little granulated sugar

Grease a Swiss roll tin measuring about 25 x 18 cm (10 x 6 inches). Heat the oven to 180°C (350°F) mark 4.

Rub the butter into the sifted flour then add the caster sugar and cinnamon and work together to form a dough.

Roll out to form a rectangle, then press into the prepared tin and smooth with a round-bladed knife. Sprinkle with chopped almonds and a little granulated sugar and bake just above the centre of the oven for 20–25 minutes, until golden brown.

Cut into fingers while still warm then leave until firm and remove carefully to a wire rack and leave until cold. Store in an airtight container.

SAVOURY BISCUITS

No book of biscuits would be complete without
a section on savoury biscuits. These are all
crisp and tasty to serve plain, with cheese or
with a savoury topping. They are also ideal
for cocktail nibbles to use with dips, or
as canapé bases.

BACON AND OATMEAL BISCUITS

Makes about 30

100 g (4 oz) hard margarine
100 g (4 oz) rolled oats
100 g (4 oz) self-raising flour
salt and pepper
1 tsp dry mustard
75–100 g (3–4 oz) lean bacon,
  finely minced
1 small egg

Heat the oven to 180°C (350°F) mark 4. Rub the margarine into the oats and sifted flour until the mixture resembles breadcrumbs. Add the salt and pepper, mustard and bacon. Mix thoroughly then add sufficient beaten egg to mix to a dough.

Roll the dough out fairly thinly on a floured board and cut into any shape required. Place on greased baking sheets and bake for 15 minutes or until golden brown. Cool on a wire rack.

CRACKAMACS

100 g (4 oz) self-raising flour
½ tsp salt
milk or water to mix

Heat the oven to 200°C (400°F) mark 6. Sift the flour and salt into a basin. Add the milk or water and mix with a fork to make a dough.

Roll the dough out very thinly on a floured board and cut into rounds or squares. Place on greased baking sheets and bake for 10–15 minutes. Cool on a wire rack. Serve with cheese.

OATCAKES

225 g (8 oz) plain flour
1 tsp salt
1 tsp bicarbonate of soda
1 tbsp caster sugar
450 g (1 lb) medium oatmeal
100 g (4 oz) margarine, melted
5 tbsp lukewarm water

Heat the oven to 190°C (375°F) mark 5. Sift the flour, salt and soda into a bowl. Mix in the sugar and oatmeal and bind together with the melted margarine and water.

Roll the dough out on a floured board to a thickness of about 2.5 mm (⅛ inch) and cut into 5-cm (2-inch) rounds. Place on greased baking sheets and bake for 20 minutes. Cool on a wire rack. These taste very good when served with cheese.

GUERNSEY BISCUITS

Makes about 40

25 g (1 oz) fresh yeast or 15 g
  (½ oz) dried yeast
15 g (½ oz) caster sugar
250 ml (8 fl oz) warm milk or water
450 g (1 lb) plain flour
15 g (½ oz) salt
100 g (4 oz) margarine

Heat the oven to 200°C (400°F) mark 6. Cream together the yeast and sugar and add the liquid (or sprinkle the dried yeast and sugar on the liquid). Leave in a warm place until frothy. Sift the flour and salt into a bowl and rub in the fat until the mixture resembles fine breadcrumbs. Add the yeast mixture to the flour and knead well. Cover and leave the dough to rise in a warm place for 1 hour.

Knock back the dough and knead again. Form into balls about 2 cm (1 inch) in diameter. Flatten the balls and roll out thinly. Place on greased baking sheets and allow them to prove for 15–20 minutes in a warm place. Bake for 20 minutes.

WHOLEMEAL SAVOURY TITBITS

Makes 8–12

100 g (4 oz) wholemeal flour
½ tsp baking powder
pinch of salt
25 g (1 oz) lard
milk to mix

Topping
4 tbsp cream cheese
1 tbsp grated cheese
1 tbsp chopped celery
salt, pepper and mustard to taste
parsley and red pepper to garnish

Heat the oven to 180°C (350°F) mark 4. For the biscuits: mix together the flour, baking powder and salt in a bowl. Rub in the lard until the mixture resembles breadcrumbs, then add sufficient milk to make a stiff dough. Roll the dough out very thinly on a floured board. Prick the dough and cut into small rounds approximately 4 cm (1½ inches) in diameter. Place on greased baking sheets and bake for 10–15 minutes until the biscuits are brown and firm. Cool on a wire rack. When they are cold, store in an airtight container.

To make the topping: mix the cream cheese, grated cheese and chopped celery. Season with salt, pepper and a little mustard. Pile this mixture on to the biscuits and garnish with sprigs of parsley and/or strips of red pepper.

PAPRIKA CHEESE BISCUITS

175 g (6 oz) plain flour
½ tsp paprika
175 g (6 oz) butter
75 g (3 oz) Cheddar cheese, finely
  grated
1 egg yolk
50 g (2 oz) unblanched almonds,
  chopped
beaten egg to glaze
extra cheese or paprika to decorate

Heat the oven to 160°C (325°F) mark 3. Sift the flour and paprika into a bowl and rub in the butter. Add the finely grated cheese and lightly beaten egg yolk. Stir in the nuts and work the mixture to a smooth dough.

Roll the dough out on a floured board to a thickness of 1 cm (½ inch). Cut into shapes with a small plain cutter and place on greased baking sheets. Brush the tops with beaten egg and sprinkle lightly with a little more cheese or paprika. Bake for about 20 minutes. Cool on a wire rack.

CHEESE STRAWS

50 g (2 oz) cheese
½ tsp salt
pinch of pepper
pinch of cayenne
75 g (3 oz) plain flour, sifted
50 g (2 oz) margarine or butter

Heat the oven to 180°C (350°F) mark 4. Rub the cheese through a wire sieve. Add the salt, pepper and cayenne to the flour. Partly cream the fat, then add the cheese and the seasoned flour. Mix it to a paste and allow to stand for at least 30 minutes, preferably in the refrigerator.

Roll the dough out on a lightly floured board and cut into straws or biscuits. Place on a greased baking sheet and prick well. Cook for about 15 minutes and cool on a wire rack.

DIGESTIVE BISCUITS

175 g (6 oz) wholewheat flour
25 g (1 oz) oatmeal
½ tsp salt
1 tsp baking powder
75 g (3 oz) butter or margarine
40 g (1½ oz) soft brown sugar
2–3 tbsp milk

Heat the oven to 190°C (375°F) mark 5. Mix together the flour and oatmeal. Sift in the salt and baking powder and rub in the fat until the mixture resembles breadcrumbs. Stir in the sugar and add sufficient milk to mix to a stiff dough.

Roll the dough out thinly on a floured board and prick well. Cut 6-cm (2½-inch) rounds with a plain cutter. Place on lightly greased baking sheets and bake for 15–20 minutes. Cool on a wire rack. Serve with cheese.

CURRY KNOTS

Makes about 18

100 g (4 oz) plain flour
2 tsp curry powder
pinch of salt
50 g (2 oz) margarine
egg yolk or water to mix
egg yolk to glaze

Heat the oven to 180°C (350°F) mark 4. Sift the flour, curry powder and salt into a bowl, and rub in the fat until the mixture resembles fine breadcrumbs. Bind the mixture to a stiff but pliable dough with a little egg yolk or water.

Knead the dough well to remove any cracks and roll it out on a floured board into a long strip about 2 cm (¾ inch) thick. Cut into 15-cm (6-inch) long pieces and tie each one into a knot. Place on a greased baking sheet and brush with beaten egg yolk. Bake for about 10–15 minutes or until golden brown. Cool on a wire rack.

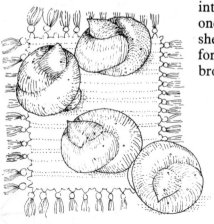

CHEESE SABLÉS

75 g (3 oz) plain flour
75 g (3 oz) butter
75 g (3 oz) cheese, grated
salt and pepper to taste
1 egg

Heat the oven to 190°C (375°F) mark 5. Sift the flour into a bowl. Cut the butter into pieces and rub into the flour. Add the grated cheese and season with the salt and pepper. Work the mixture together to make a dough. Wrap the dough in greaseproof paper or foil and chill in the refrigerator for about 30 minutes.

Roll out the dough carefully on a floured board until it is fairly thin. Cut into strips about 5 cm (2 inches) wide and brush with the lightly beaten egg. Cut the strips into triangles and place on a baking sheet lined with greaseproof paper. Bake for 10 minutes until the biscuits are golden brown. Cool on a wire rack.

WALNUT SAVOURY BISCUITS

175 g (6 oz) plain flour
½ tsp salt
½ tsp dry mustard
pinch of pepper
50 g (2 oz) rolled oats
75 g (3 oz) margarine
75 g (3 oz) Cheddar cheese, grated
50 g (2 oz) walnuts, chopped
1 egg
150 ml (¼ pint) cold water
a few chopped nuts to garnish

Sift together the flour, salt, mustard and pepper, add the oats and rub in the margarine until the mixture resembles breadcrumbs. Stir in the grated cheese and walnuts. Beat the egg and reserve a teaspoonful for the glaze. Add the remaining egg to the mixture and bind to a stiff dough with sufficient water.

Roll out the mixture on a floured board and trim to make a rectangle. Add a pinch of salt to the remaining egg and brush over the surface. Sprinkle the top with a few chopped nuts. Cut into shapes and place on greased baking sheets. Bake for 12–15 minutes. Cool on a wire rack.

CHEESE BISCUITS

225 g (8 oz) plain flour
1 tsp baking powder
good pinch of salt
pinch of cayenne
75 g (3 oz) butter
225 g (8 oz) cheese, grated
1 egg yolk
cold water

Heat the oven to 200°C (400°F) mark 6. Sift the flour, baking powder, salt and cayenne into a bowl. Rub in the butter, until the mixture resembles fine breadcrumbs. Stir in the cheese. Beat the egg yolk with a little cold water, add to the rest of the ingredients and mix to form a stiff dough.

Knead lightly on a floured board, roll out thinly and cut into rounds. Place on greased baking sheets and bake for 10–15 minutes until a pale golden brown. Cool on a wire rack.

CHEESE CRACKERS

100 g (4 oz) self-raising flour
pinch of salt
25 g (1 oz) cheese, finely grated
cold water
50 g (2 oz) butter or margarine

Heat the oven to 160°C (325°F) mark 3. Sift the flour and salt into a bowl, then add the finely grated cheese. Mix to a firm dough with the cold water and knead the mixture until it is smooth.

Roll the dough out into an oblong 23 x 12.5 cm (9 x 5 inches) and mark lightly into three portions. Spread 25 g (1 oz) of the butter over the top two-thirds of the dough. Fold the unbuttered portion upwards and top third downwards, envelope fashion. Give the dough a half-turn, and roll it out again, a little larger than the original oblong. Repeat the process with the remainder of the butter, and fold it again. Cover and put in a cool place for 30 minutes.

Roll the dough out and fold it once more (with no fat), then roll it out thinly to less than 5 mm (¼ inch) thick. Cut into squares. Place on lightly greased baking sheets, prick all over and bake for 15–20 minutes. Cool on a wire rack.

CELERY BISCUITS

225 g (8 oz) plain flour
pinch of salt
50 g (2 oz) margarine
2 tsp celery seeds
top of the milk or single cream

Heat the oven to 200°C (400°F) mark 6. Sift the flour and salt into a bowl. Rub in the fat until the mixture resembles fine breadcrumbs then add the celery seeds. Add sufficient liquid to mix to a stiff, pliable dough. Knead thoroughly, roll out thinly on a floured board and cut into rounds. Place on greased baking sheets and bake for 10–15 minutes. Cool the biscuits on a wire rack.

Serve alone, with butter or cheese, or with both.

SAVOURY CURLS

Makes about 40

50 g (2 oz) margarine
1 rounded tsp Marmite
100 g (4 oz) plain flour, sieved
40 g (1½ oz) cheese, grated
water to mix

Heat the oven to 200°C (400°F) mark 6. Blend the margarine and Marmite together and leave in a cool place for about 15 minutes. Rub the creamed mixture into the flour and add the cheese. Mix to a stiff dough with a little water.

Roll out to a rectangle about 15 cm x 20 cm (6 x 8 inches) and cut into strips about 1 cm (½ inch) wide. Cut each strip into two and twist slightly. Place on greased baking sheets and bake for 5–8 minutes until pale golden brown. Cool on wire racks.

CREAM CRACKERS

450 g (1 lb) plain flour
1 tsp baking powder
pinch of salt
100 g (4 oz) butter or lard
water or milk to mix

Heat the oven to 180°C (350°F) mark 4. Sift the flour, salt and baking powder into a bowl. Rub in the butter until the mixture resembles breadcrumbs. Add sufficient water or milk to make a stiff dough.

Roll out very thinly indeed and cut into squares. Place on greased baking sheets and prick well. Bake for about 20 minutes until crisp. Cool on a wire rack.

Serve spread with butter and thinly spread with Marmite, sandwiched together.

RED CHEESE BISCUITS

50 g (2 oz) red cheese, grated
50 g (2 oz) margarine
50 g (2 oz) plain flour

Heat the oven to 180°C (350°F) mark 4. Rub the margarine and cheese into the flour until a firm paste is formed. No liquid need be added. Roll out very thinly and cut into shapes. Place on a greased baking sheet and bake in the centre of the oven for 5–7 minutes. Cool on a wire rack.

CHEESE WAFERS

50 g (2 oz) butter
50 g (2 oz) cheese, grated
100 g (4 oz) plain flour
pinch of salt
pinch of dry mustard
½ tsp Worcestershire sauce
salt for sprinkling

Heat the oven to 190°C (375°F) mark 5. Cream together the butter and grated cheese. Sieve together the flour and seasonings and work into the creamed mixture with a fork. Add the Worcestershire sauce and knead lightly to form a smooth, firm dough.

Roll out thinly and cut into small squares or rounds. Place on a greased baking sheet and bake for about 8–10 minutes in the centre of the oven. Sprinkle with salt while hot. Cool on a wire rack.

SAVOURY COCONUT TOASTIES

Makes 24

50 g (2 oz) plain flour
pinch of cayenne pepper
pinch of salt
pinch of cinnamon
100 g (4 oz) Cheddar cheese, grated
50 g (2 oz) coconut, toasted
1 egg, separated

Heat the oven to 200°C (400°F) mark 6. Sift the flour, cayenne, salt and cinnamon into a bowl. Add the cheese, coconut and egg yolk and mix all together. Whisk the egg white until stiff and fold into the mixture. Form teaspoonfuls into pyramids and place on well greased baking sheets. Bake for 10 minutes. Cool on wire racks or serve hot.

CHEESE AND TOMATO BISCUITS

50 g (2 oz) margarine
100 g (4 oz) plain flour, sifted
50 g (2 oz) cheese, grated
2 tbsp tomato sauce, preferably
    homemade
water to mix

Filling
cheese spread or cream cheese

Heat the oven to 200°C (400°F) mark 6. Rub the margarine into the flour until the mixture resembles fine breadcrumbs. Add the grated cheese and the tomato sauce and mix to a stiff dough.

Roll out and cut into shapes as desired. Place on a greased baking sheet and bake for 10–15 minutes. Cool on a wire rack.

When cold, sandwich together with cheese spread or cream cheese.

WHAT IS THE WI ?

If you have enjoyed this book, the chances are that you would enjoy belonging to the largest women's organisation in the country — the Women's Institutes.

We are friendly, go-ahead, like-minded women, who derive enormous satisfaction from all the movement has to offer. This list is long — you can make new friends, have fun and companionship, visit new places, develop new skills, take part in community services, fight local campaigns, become a WI market producer, and play an active role in an organisation which has a national voice.

The WI is the only women's organisation in the country which owns an adult education establishment. At Denman College, you can take a course in anything from car maintenance to paper sculpture, from book binding to yoga, or cordon bleu cookery to fly-fishing.

All you need to do to join is write to us here at the **National Federation of Women's Institutes, 39 Eccleston Street, London SW1W 9NT**, or telephone 01-730 7212, and we will put you in touch with WIs in your immediate locality. We hope to hear from you.

Biscuits for shows
Please note that if you wish to enter homemade biscuits in a show, it is important to check the schedule first with regard to the quantity and variety. Biscuits, by definition, should be crisp; they should be even in size and colour, of a good shape and not too thick.

Some of the recipes in this book may not be accepted by judges for shows because they may not all fall within the definitions of the schedule.

INDEX

Abbey Biscuits, 48
Almond
  Balls, 66
  Bars, 56
  Biscuits, 62
  Biscuits, German, 78
  Butter Crisps, 54
  Cocoroons, 65
  Jumbles, 65
  paste, 55
  see also Wholemeal
  Shortcake
Alphabet Biscuits, 7
Anzac Cookies, 50
Appleby Fairings, 69
Apricot Shortcakes, 18
Auntie Dot's Biscuits, 28

Bacon and Oatmeal
  Biscuits, 83
Basic Drop Cookies, 18
Belgian Sugar
  Biscuits, 74
Blantyre Biscuits, 46
Bourbon Biscuits, 76
Brandy Cornets, 76
Bufton Biscuits, 50
Burnt Butter Biscuits, 22
Butter
  Cookies, 28
  Crisps, Almond, 54
  Knots, 64
  see also Burnt Butter
  Biscuits

Caramel
  Biscuits, 36
  Rolls, Orange, 67
Caraway Biscuits, 9
Caraway Moments, 19
Cardamom Cookies, 60
Catherine Wheels, 35
Celery Biscuits, 89

Cheese
  and Tomato
  Biscuits, 91
  Biscuits, 88
  Biscuits, Paprika, 85
  Biscuits, Red, 90
  Crackers, 88
  Sablés, 87
  Straws, 85
  Wafers, 90
Cherry
  and Chocolate
  Chews, 40
  Biscuits, Chocolate, 40
  Snowballs, 56
  Whirls, 10
  see also Coconut and
  Cherry Slice
Chestnut Biscuits, 24
Chocolate
  Biscuits, 37
  Cherry Biscuits, 40
  Chip Biscuits, 35
  Coconut Kisses, 42
  Nut Biscuits, 57
  Oat Biscuits, 49
  Peppermint Creams,
  38
  Quickies, 38
  Stars, 39
  Wafers, 19
  Wagon Wheels, 40
Christmas Tree
  Cookies, 30
Cinnamon
  Bars, 24
  Wafers, 18
  see also Kelvin Crisps

Coconut
  and Cherry Slices, 37
  Biscuits, 10
  Butter Biscuits, 28
  Crisps, 15
  Crisps, Orange, 8
  Drops, 26
  Kisses, 7
  Kisses, Chocolate, 42
  Rings, 22
  Toasties, Savoury, 91
  Wafers, 32
Coffee
  Cookies, 17
  Kisses, 12
cornflakes, *see* Gipsy
  Crisps
Cornish Ginger
  Fairings, 69
Coupland Biscuits, 45
Crackamacs, 83
Cream Crackers, 90
Crescent Biscuits, 59
Creston Drops, 59
Crisps, 22
  see also Orange and
  Coconut Crisps
Crunchies, 48
Crunchy Biscuits, 30
Cumberland Snaps, 47
Curly Peters, 39
Curry Knots, 86

Danish Specier
  Biscuits, 72
Date Slices, 51
Date Sticks, 53
Digestive Biscuits, 86
Dream Cookies, 27
Drop Cookies, 36
  see also Basic Drop
  Cookies
Dutch Janhagel, 81

Easter Biscuits, 73
Easter Bunny
   Biscuits, 13

Fairings, *see* Cornish
   Ginger Fairings,
   Appleby Fairings
Finnish Shortbread, 75
Firelighter Biscuits, 46
Flaked Almond
   Biscuits, 48
Florentines, 70
   see also Quick
   Florentines
Freezer Biscuits, 20
Fruit and Nut
   Cookies, 18
Fruited Ginger
   Biscuits, 32
Fruity Brittles, 58
Fruity Snaps, 17
Fudge Biscuits, Lemon,
   27

Garibaldi Biscuits, 71
German Almond
   Biscuits, 78
German Biscuits, 77
Ginger
   Biscuits, 19
   Drops, Grantham, 72
   Fairings, Cornish, 69
   Ruffles, 13
   Shortcake, Iced, 11
   Snaps, 14
   see also Fruited Ginger
   Biscuits
Gingerbread,
   Grasmere, 72
Gipsy Creams, 43
Gipsy Crisps, 8
Grantham Ginger
   Drops, 72

Grasmere Gingerbread,
   72
Ground Rice Cookies, 8
Guernsey Biscuits, 84

Hazelnut
   Biscuits, 55
   Crunchies, 66
Highlanders, 11
Honey Biscuits, 26

Iced Ginger Shortcake, 11
Iced Peppermint
   Biscuits, 41
Iced Raspberry Biscuits,
   20
icing, 7, 11, 17, 20, 27,
   41, 55, 77

Janhagel, Dutch, 81
Jumbles, 75

Kelvin Crisps, 25
Kichelech, 80
   see also Quick
   Kichelech
King Haakon
   Biscuits, 60
Kipferl, Vanilla, 61
Kisses,
   Coconut, 7
   Coffee, 12
Kourabiédes, 70
Kringles, 29

Lace Biscuits, 58
Lancashire Nuts, 71
Lemon
   Crescents, 12
   Fudge Biscuits, 27
   see also Rich Biscuits

Macaroons, 69

Macaroonies, 67
Ma'moule, 62
Marzipan Biscuits, 60
measurements, 5
Melting Moments, 51
Meringues, Passover, 81
Muesli Biscuits,
   Chocolate, 42

Napoleon Biscuits, 9
Napoleon Hats, 55
Novelty Biscuits, 10
Nut and Fruit
   Shortbread, 57

Oat Biscuits, 45
   see also Chocolate Oat
   Biscuits, Peppermint
   Oat Biscuits, Rolled
   Oat Biscuits
Oatcakes, 83
Oatmeal Biscuits, 26
   see also Bacon and
   Oatmeal Biscuits
Orange
   Caramel Rolls, 67
   Coconut Crisps, 8
   Creams, 14
   Meltaways, 31

Paprika Cheese
   Biscuits, 85
Passover Meringues, 81
Peanut Butter
   Cookies, 15
Peanut Cookies, 54
Peppermint
   Biscuits, Iced, 41
   Creams, Chocolate, 35
   Oat Biscuits, 49
Petits Fours, 63
Pineapple Buttons, 31

Pyramid Biscuits, *see*
  Semolina Pyramid
  Biscuits

Quick Florentines, 42
Quick Kichelech, 80

Raisin Shortcake, 21
Raspberry Biscuits,
  Iced, 20
Red Cheese Biscuits, 90
Rice Biscuits, 15
  see also Ground Rice
  Cookies
Rich Biscuits, 16
Rolled Oat Biscuits, 45

Savoury Biscuits,
  Walnut, 87
Savoury Coconut
  Toasties, 91
Savoury Curls, 89
Semolina Pyramid
  Biscuits, 24
Shortbread Biscuits, 78
  see also Finnish
  Shortbread, Nut and
  Fruit Shortbread
Shortcake
  Wholemeal, 27
  see also Iced Ginger
  Shortcake, Raisin
  Shortcake
Shortcakes, Apricot, 18
Specier Biscuits,
  Danish, 72
Strawberry Delights, 64
Sugar Biscuits,
  Belgian, 74
Sweetmeal Cookies, 16

Tebay Crunch, 46
Tuiles, 79

Vanilla Kipferl, 61
Viennese Biscuits, 74

Walnut
  Bars, 53
  Biscuits, Coffee, 54
  Crisps, 53
  Savoury Biscuits, 87
  see also Novelty
  Biscuits
Wholemeal
  Savoury Titbits, 84
  Shortcake, 27
  see also Sweetmeal
  Cookies

Yo-Yo's, 23